# JAZZ
## CHORD PROGRESSIONS
### by Bill Boyd

ISBN 978-0-7935-7038-6

**HAL•LEONARD®**
**CORPORATION**
7777 W. BLUEMOUND RD. P.O. BOX 13819 MILWAUKEE, WI 53213

Visit Hal Leonard on the internet at http://www.halleonard.com

# FOREWORD

This book contains the chord progressions found in most jazz standards. Each progression is written with chord voicings which are indigenous to the style.

The book is divided into two sections. The first section uses chord voicings with the root as the bottom note. This voicing is appropriate when playing with a jazz group where there is no bass player. Chord voicings with the third or seventh of the chord as the bottom note are the basis for section two. This voicing is useful when a bass player is present to provide the root movement. The same progressions appear in both sections.

The study of this material will help prepare the player for fake book reading and comping with a group.

# JAZZ CHORD PROGRESSIONS

# CONTENTS

# 1. INTRODUCTION

All chord voicings and progressions are written out completely.  However, it will be easier to understand the material and apply it to practical playing situations if the reader has a knowledge of chord construction and is able to play root postion chords in all keys.

## CHORD CONSTRUCTION

A quick review of chord construction follows.  Chords are constructed by formula from the notes of the major scale.  The first thirteen notes of the major scale are used for chord construction.

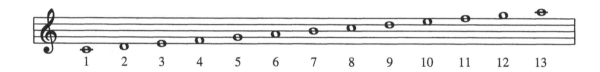

The first note of the chord is called the ROOT.  It is the note for which the chord is named.  In the examples below, the chord name appears followed by the formula and the notation of the chord on the staff.  The letter over the chord is the CHORD SYMBOL.

A TRIAD is a three-note chord.

The sixth note above the root may be added.

The seventh note above the root may be added.  Sometimes the seventh is flatted.

The top note of a diminished seventh chord is a double flat seventh.  It is easier to think of this note as six notes above the root.

Notes may be added which are nine, eleven and thirteen notes above the root.

The fifth, ninth and eleventh may be altered (♭ or ♯).

The m7♭5 chord is sometimes called a half diminished.
Chord symbol: ø

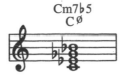

Suspended chords include the fourth note above the root in place of the third.

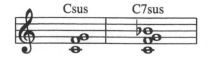

Chords may be placed within the context of a key. A chord is built on each scale step. Roman numerals which correspond to the scale steps serve as chord symbols.

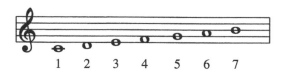

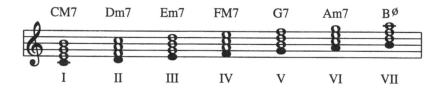

# II V I

When one chord moves to another, the movement is called a CHORD PROGRESSION. The II V I chord progression is one of the most important in jazz harmony. Study the charts below and memorize this progression.

<table>
<tr><td colspan="4">MAJOR KEYS</td><td colspan="4">MINOR KEYS</td></tr>
<tr><td>KEY</td><td>IIm7</td><td>V7</td><td>I</td><td>KEY</td><td>IIm7♭5</td><td>V7</td><td>Im</td></tr>
<tr><td>C</td><td>Dm7</td><td>G7</td><td>C</td><td>Cm</td><td>Dm7♭5</td><td>G7</td><td>Cm</td></tr>
<tr><td>D♭</td><td>E♭m7</td><td>A♭7</td><td>D♭</td><td>D♭m</td><td>E♭m7♭5</td><td>A♭7</td><td>D♭m</td></tr>
<tr><td>D</td><td>Em7</td><td>A7</td><td>D</td><td>Dm</td><td>Em7♭5</td><td>A7</td><td>Dm</td></tr>
<tr><td>E♭</td><td>Fm7</td><td>B♭7</td><td>E♭</td><td>E♭m</td><td>Fm7♭5</td><td>B♭7</td><td>E♭m</td></tr>
<tr><td>E</td><td>F♯m7</td><td>B7</td><td>E</td><td>Em</td><td>F♯m7♭5</td><td>B7</td><td>Em</td></tr>
<tr><td>F</td><td>Gm7</td><td>C7</td><td>F</td><td>Fm</td><td>Gm7♭5</td><td>C7</td><td>Fm</td></tr>
<tr><td>G♭</td><td>A♭m7</td><td>D♭7</td><td>G♭</td><td>G♭m</td><td>A♭m7♭5</td><td>D♭7</td><td>G♭m</td></tr>
<tr><td>G</td><td>Am7</td><td>D7</td><td>G</td><td>Gm</td><td>Am7♭5</td><td>D7</td><td>Gm</td></tr>
<tr><td>A♭</td><td>B♭m7</td><td>E♭7</td><td>A♭</td><td>A♭m</td><td>B♭m7♭5</td><td>E♭7</td><td>A♭m</td></tr>
<tr><td>A</td><td>Bm7</td><td>E7</td><td>A</td><td>Am</td><td>Bm7♭5</td><td>E7</td><td>Am</td></tr>
<tr><td>B♭</td><td>Cm7</td><td>F7</td><td>B♭</td><td>B♭m</td><td>Cm7♭5</td><td>F7</td><td>B♭m</td></tr>
<tr><td>B</td><td>C♯m7</td><td>F♯7</td><td>B</td><td>Bm</td><td>C♯m7♭5</td><td>F♯7</td><td>Bm</td></tr>
</table>

# THE CHORD VOICINGS

Chord voicing refers to the way in which the notes of the chord are distributed between the two hands. Voicings are presented for all forms of the C chord. Labels indicate the chord tone distribution.

# THE CHORD PROGRESSIONS

The chord progressions are a composite of many standard jazz tunes. Each progression is preceded by a "fake book form" version. Fake book form is a single staff with the basic chord symbols written above. Only the melody is missing. Fake books do not always include extended or altered chords. The extended and altered chords are included in the chord progression examples.

Play each chord progression in all of the written keys in order to recognize the progression when it appears in a song. In addition, this practice will improve your ability to transpose.

The examples should be played as written. However, the chord progressions are presented in a format which may be adapted to group playing. The keyboard player is often required to provide an accompaniment for a soloist. This accompaniment style is called COMPING. Comping is the jazz vernacular for accompanying. In order to adapt the exercise to comping style, various rhythm patterns may be added.

**ORIGINAL VERSION:**

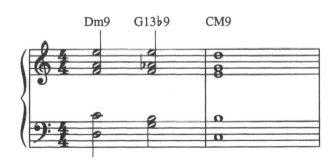

**COMPING VERSION:**

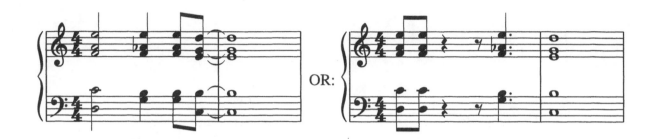

OR:

# THE TRI-TONE SUBSTITUTION

Chords in a progression may be replaced with other chords. These "replacements" are referred to as SUBSTITUTE chords. The most common substitution is called the tri-tone substitution.

The distance between two tones which are three whole steps apart is an augmented fourth. This distance is often called a TRI-TONE.

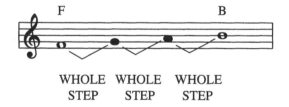

WHOLE   WHOLE   WHOLE
STEP    STEP    STEP

Any two dominant seventh chords whose roots are a tri-tone apart will substitute for one another. The preceding example illustrates that F7 will substitute for B7 and B7 will substitute for F7.

Memorize:

| | |
|---|---|
| F7 substitutes for B7 | subs for F7 |
| E7 substitutes for B♭7 | subs for E7 |
| E♭7 substitutes for A7 | subs for E♭7 |
| D7 substitutes for A♭7 | subs for D7 |
| D♭7 substitutes for G7 | subs for D♭7 |
| C7 substitutes for G♭7 | subs for C7 |

The six tri-tone substitutions are written below. The right hand notes are the same for both chords; only the roots change.

II V I with the tri-tone substitution follows. The Db7 chord substitutes for the G7 chord in the second example.

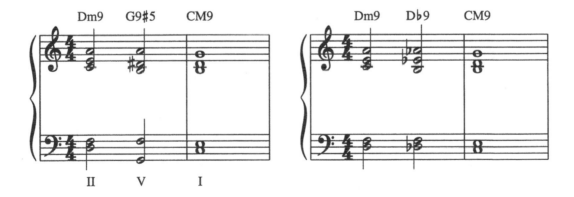

The text will always indicate when a tri-tone substitution appears in the chord progression.

# 2. CHORD VOICINGS WITH THE ROOT AS THE BOTTOM NOTE

## POSITION 1

The third of the chord is the bottom note in the right hand in Position 1. The C chord serves to illustrate the various chord types.

**MAJOR:**

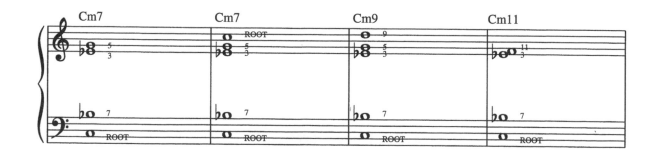

**MINOR:**

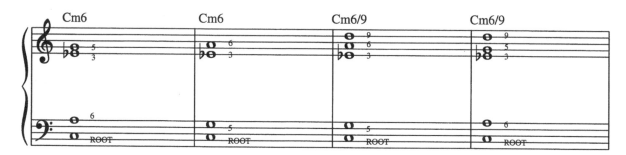

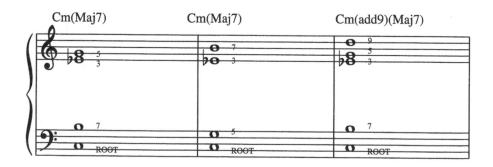

**DOMINANT SEVENTH:**

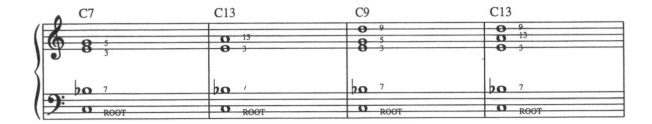

**DIMINISHED:**

## ALTERED CHORDS

**MAJOR:**

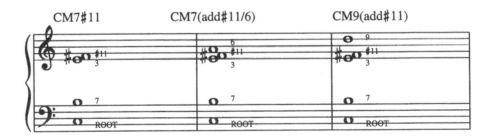

**MINOR:**

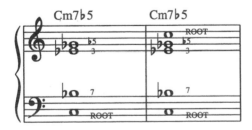

**DOMINANT SEVENTH:**

When more than one note is altered the abbreviation for the word "altered" may appear in the chord symbol.

C7 alt.

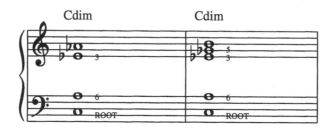

## DIMINISHED:

Sometimes the note which is one whole step above the 5th or 6th is played with the diminished 7th chord.  In measure one below, the "A♭" is a whole step above the 5th and in measure two the "B" is one whole step above the 6th.

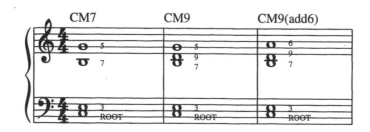

# POSITION 2

The seventh of the chord is the bottom note in the right hand in Position 2.
## MAJOR:

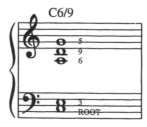

The second example above is an exception to the rule.  Notice that the bottom note of the right hand is the sixth.

## MINOR:

6th is lowest note in R.H.

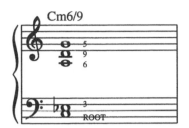 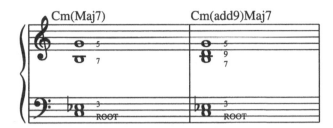

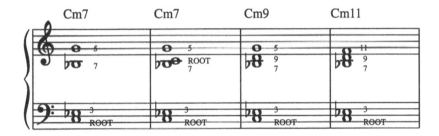 

## DOMINANT SEVENTH:

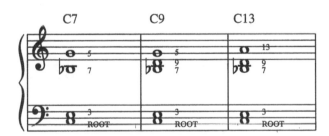

## DIMINISHED:

The sixth is the bottom note in the right hand in the example above.

# ALTERED CHORDS

**MAJOR:**

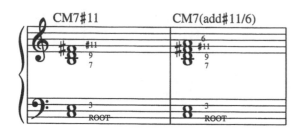

**MINOR:**

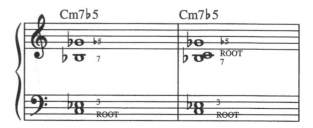

## DOMINANT SEVENTH:

Any chord containing the ♭5 may be written as a ♯11.

## DIMINISHED:

The sixth is the bottom note in the right hand.  In this position the note which is one whole step above the root is addded.

# 3. CHORD PROGRESSIONS

The Position 1 and Position 2 chord voicings are applied to chord progressions.  The selection of position is determined by the root movement.

| ROOT MOVEMENT | CHORD POSITION |
|---|---|
| 1.  Remains the same | same position |
| 2.  4th or 5th | alternate positions |
| 3.  3rd or 6th | either position or nearest position |
| 4.  2nd or 1/2 step | maintain the same position |

Examples of the various root movements are illustrated below.  The positions (P.1 or P.2) are indicated in the middle of the staff.

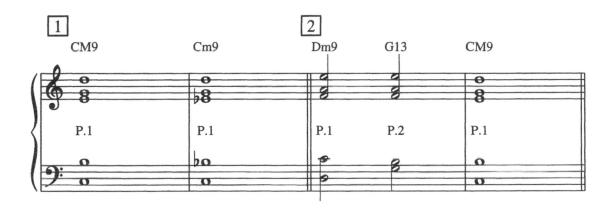

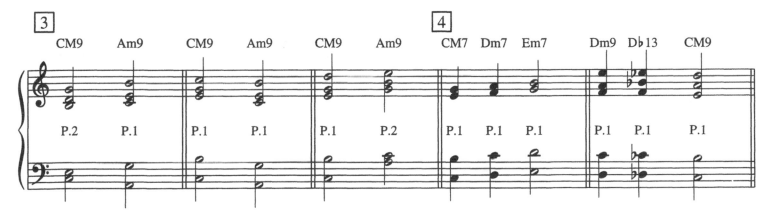

For the best sound, the voicings should fall within the range indicated below.

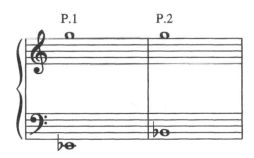

Sometimes if the position rules are followed, the voicings become too low or high (Example 1 below). There are two ways of avoiding this situation. One alternative is to switch positions in the middle of the progression (Ex. 2 below). Another choice is to begin the progression with the alternate position (Ex. 3).

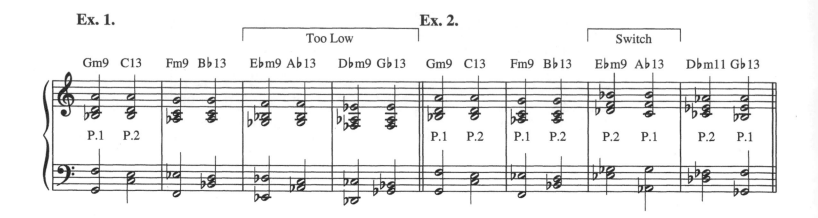

**Ex. 3.**

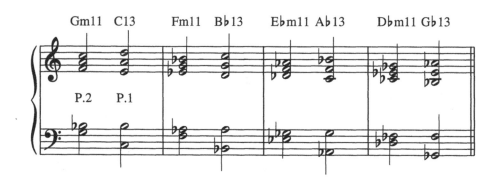

The first chord progression is II V I in all major keys. Memorize this progression as it will help prepare for the other chord progressions which follow. Each progression is first presented in "fake book form" in the key of C.

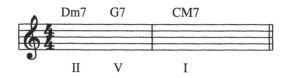

Beginning with Position 1:

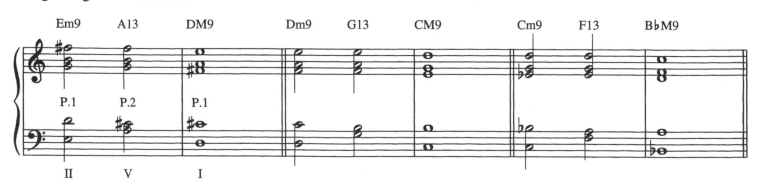

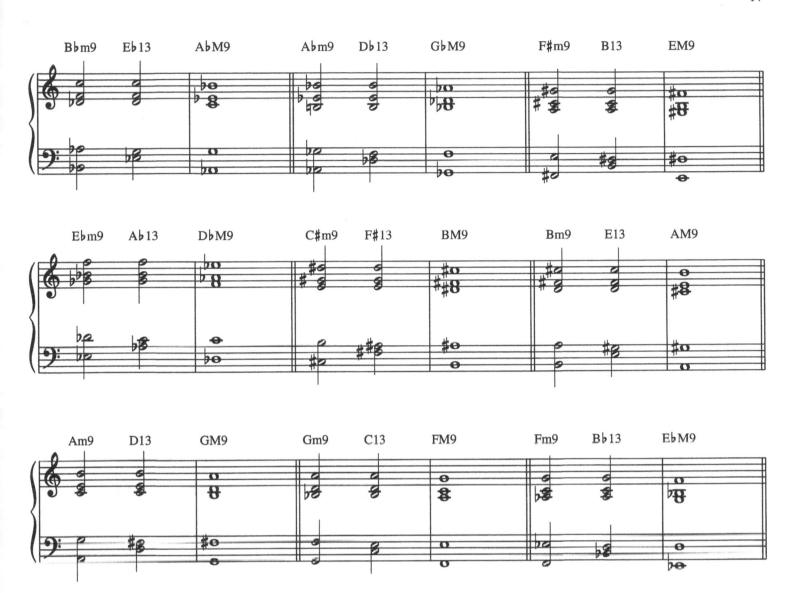

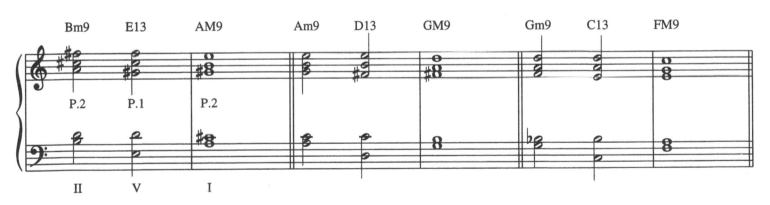

Beginning with Position 2:

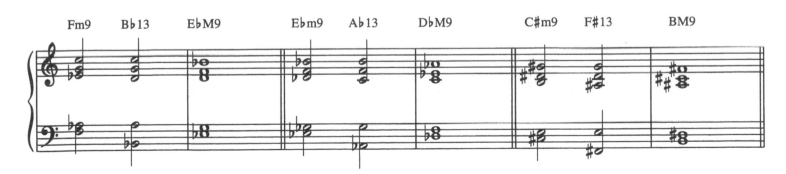

The next chord progression is a series of dominant 7th chords. This progression often appears as the bridge in standard jazz tunes. The chord voicings are in the seven keys in which most jazz standards are written.

Beginning with Position I:

**KEY: G**

**C**

**F**

A13      D13      G13      C13

**B♭**

D13      G13      C13      F13

**E♭**

G13      C13      F13      B♭13

**A♭**

C13      F13      B♭13      E♭13

**D♭**

F13      B♭13      E♭13      A♭13

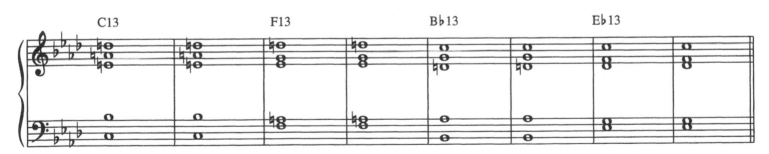

Beginning with Position 2:

**G**

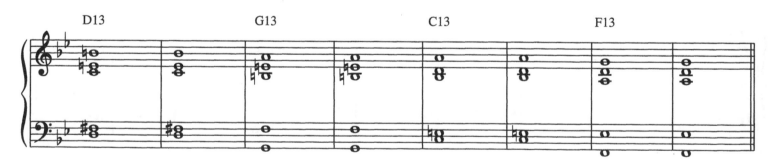

**C**

**F**

**B♭**

**E♭**

**A♭**

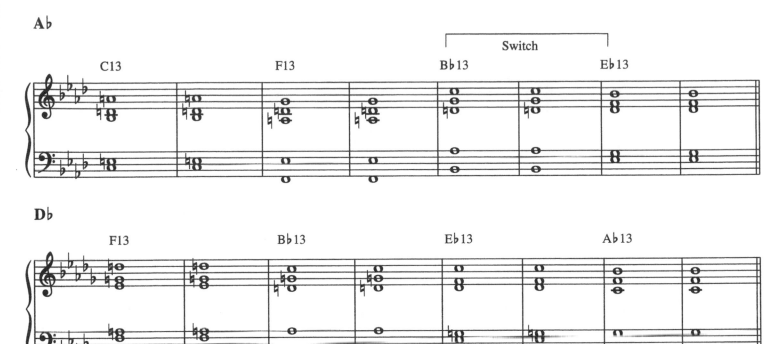

**D♭**

The following chord progression is the same as the preceding one. However, m7 chords have been placed before each dominant 7th chord to establish a temporary II V relationship. This makes the chord progression more interesting.

Fake book chord symbols often express the chord in its most simple form. In practical playing situations extended and altered chords are played. In the following chord progression m7 chords become m9 or m11 and dominant 7th chords contain 9ths, 13ths and altered notes.

Starting with Position 1:

**KEY: G**

**C**

**F**

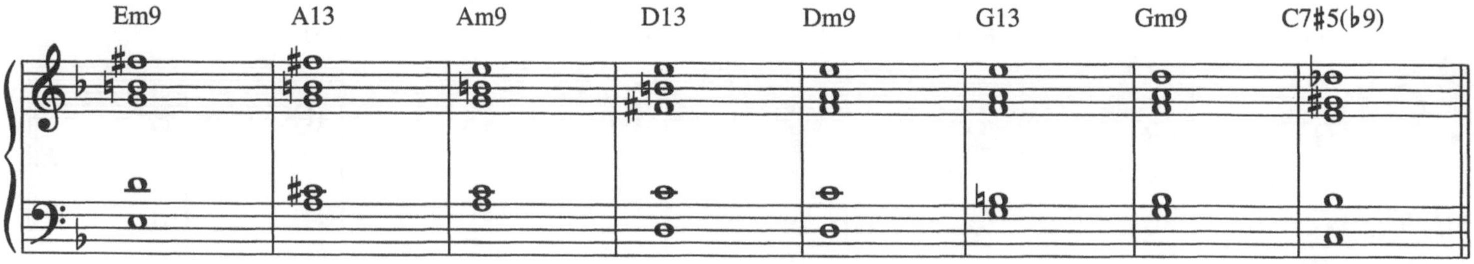
Em9
A13
Am9
D13
Dm9
G13
Gm9
C7#5(b9)

**B♭**

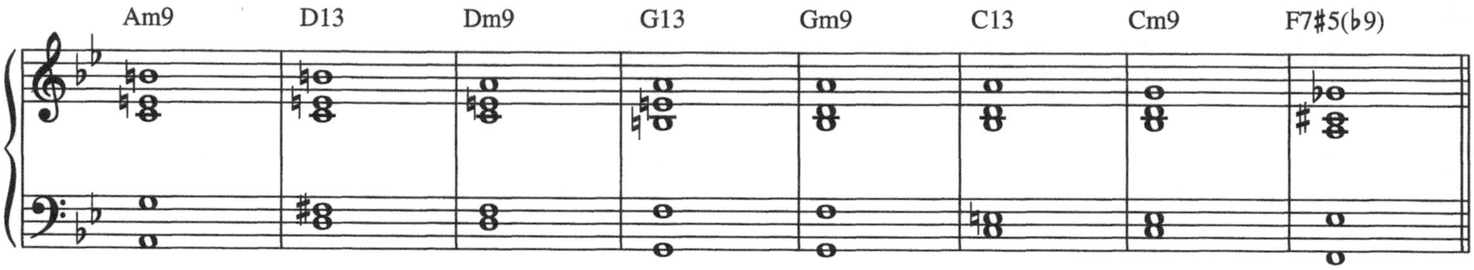
Am9
D13
Dm9
G13
Gm9
C13
Cm9
F7#5(b9)

**E♭**

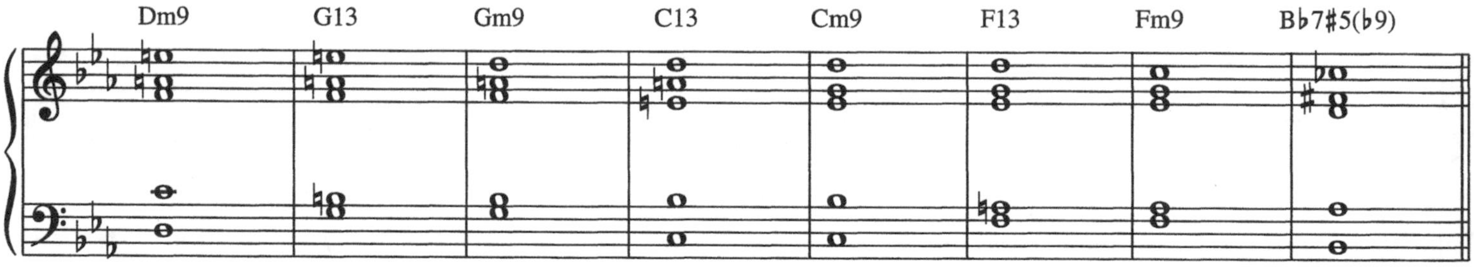
Dm9
G13
Gm9
C13
Cm9
F13
Fm9
Bb7#5(b9)

**A♭**

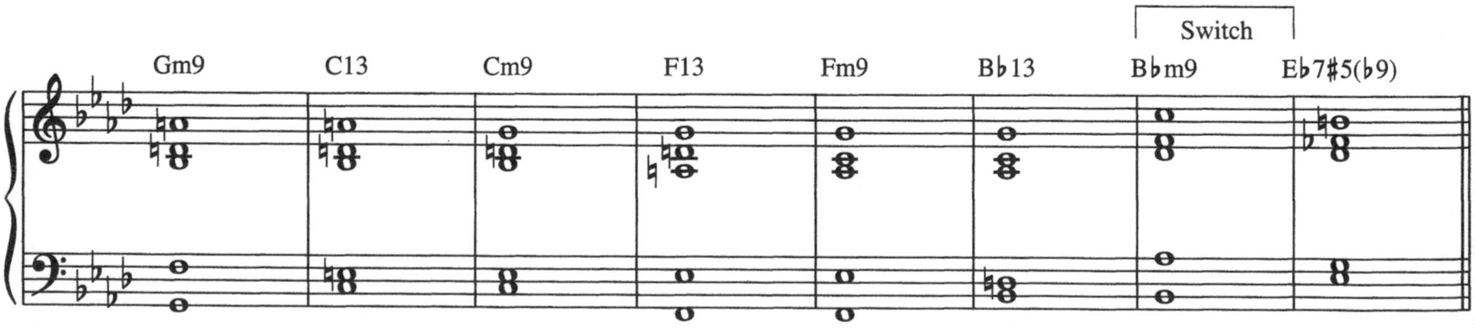
Switch
Gm9
C13
Cm9
F13
Fm9
Bb13
Bbm9
Eb7#5(b9)

**D♭**

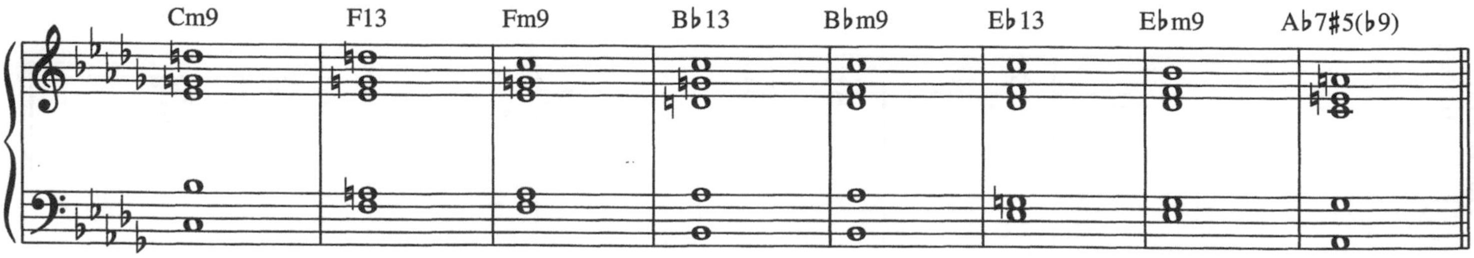
Cm9
F13
Fm9
Bb13
Bbm9
Eb13
Ebm9
Ab7#5(b9)

Starting with Position 2:

**Key: G**

F#m11 · B13 · Bm9 · E13 · Em11 · A13 · Am9 · D13♭9

P.2 · P.1 · P.1 · P.2 · P.2 · P.1 · P.1 · P.2

**C**

Bm11 · E13 · Em9 · A13 · Am11 · D13 · Dm9 · G13♭9

**F**

Em11 · A13 · Am9 · D13 · Dm11 · G13 · Gm9 · C13♭9

**B♭**

Am11 · D13 · Dm9 · G13 · Gm11 · C13 · Cm9 · F13♭9

**E♭**

Dm11 · G13 · Gm9 · C13 · Cm11 · F13 · Fm9 · B♭13♭9

**A♭**

**D♭**

Sometimes the same chord may be indicated for four measures.

Any voicing assigned to a chord may be embellished by chords a half step above or below that chord. This device also works well on chord progressions of shorter duration. The added chords should be played quickly and on weak beats. The chord progression above may be played in the following manner:

The next progression with diminished 7th chords combines 4 and 5 note voicings.  In addition, the tri-tone substitution is applied to the A7 and G7 chords.  (See Chapter 1)

Starting with Position 1:

**KEY: G**

**E♭**

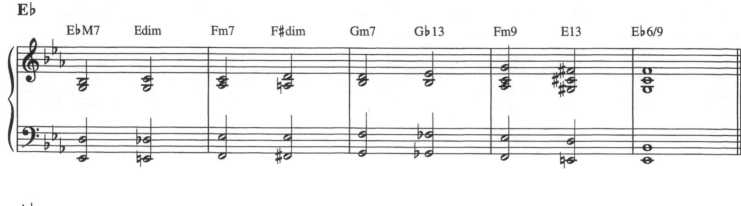

**A♭**

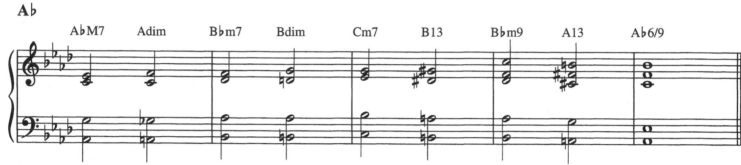

**D♭**

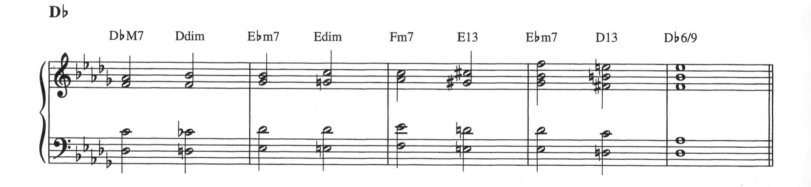

Starting with Position 2:

**KEY: G**

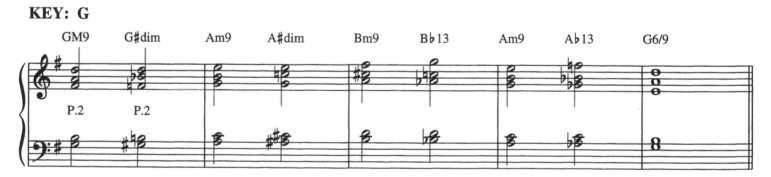

**C**

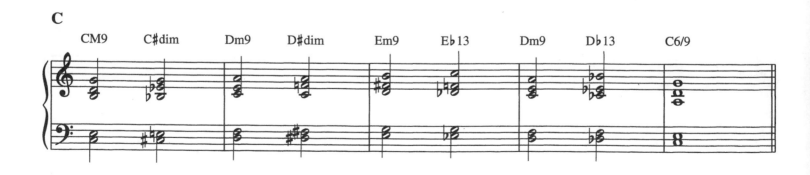

**F**

**B♭**

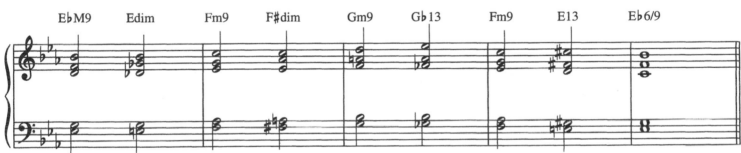

**E♭**

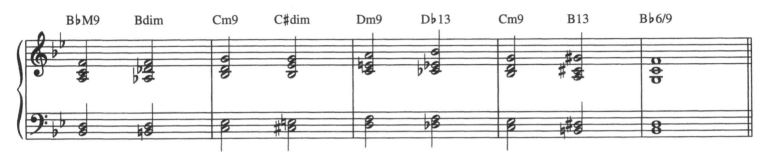

**A♭**

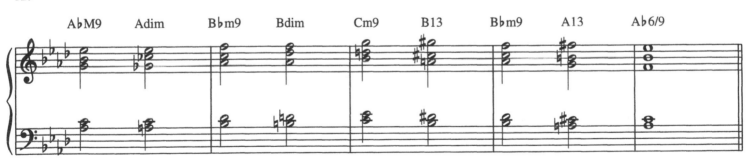

**D♭**

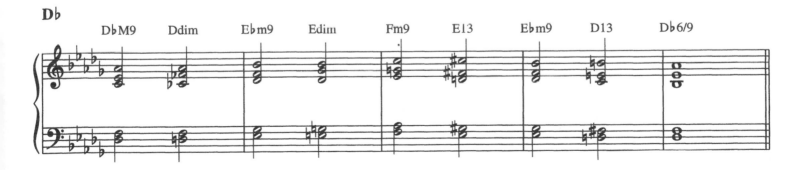

28

In order to facilitate reading, the chord progressions in the remainder of this book are written with no key signatures and some notes are written enharmonically. The keys are indicated but all accidentals are written. The reader should be aware of the key when playing the progression.

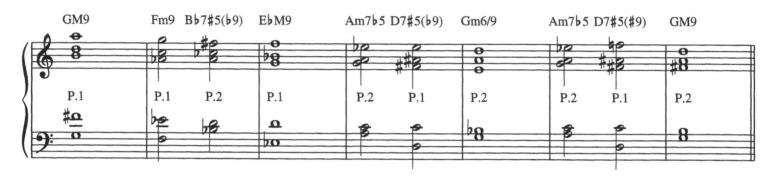

Starting with Position 1:

**KEY: G**

C

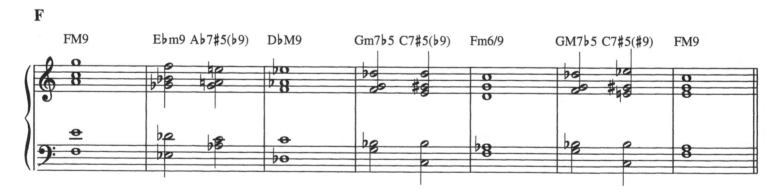

F

B♭

**Eb**

**Starting with Position 2:**

**G**

**C**

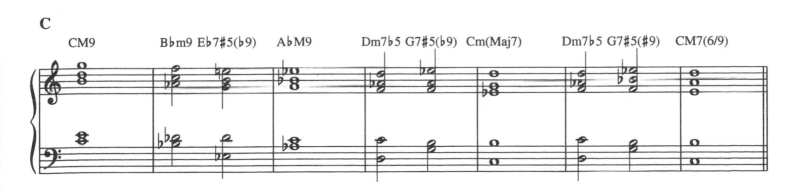

**F**

**B♭**

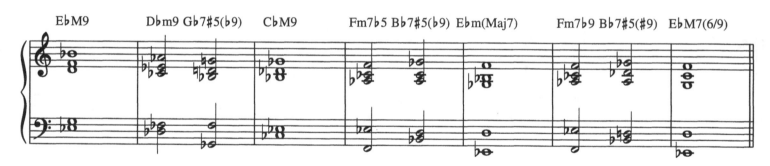

**E♭**

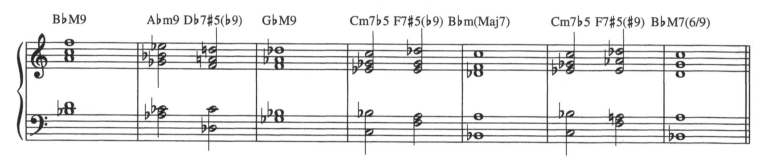

**A♭**

**D♭**

The next progression combines 4, 5 and 6 note voicings. This combination technique helps to create a more melodic top voice throughout the progression.

Starting with Position 1:

**Eb**

**Ab**

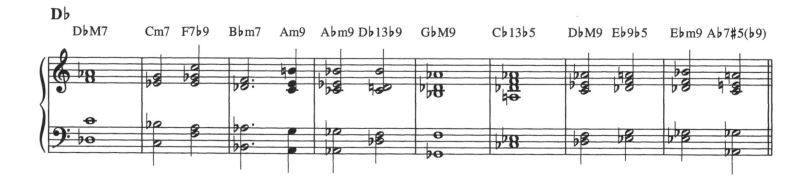

**Db**

Starting with Position 2: Notice the descending top voice.

**G**

**C**

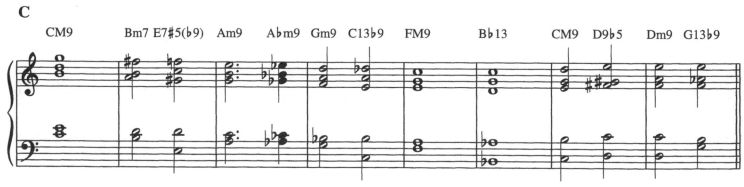

Starting with Position 1:

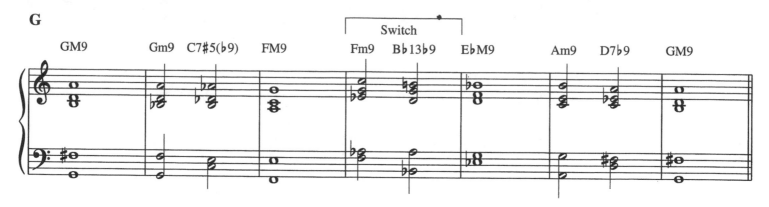

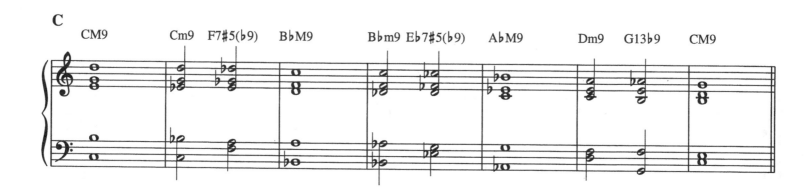

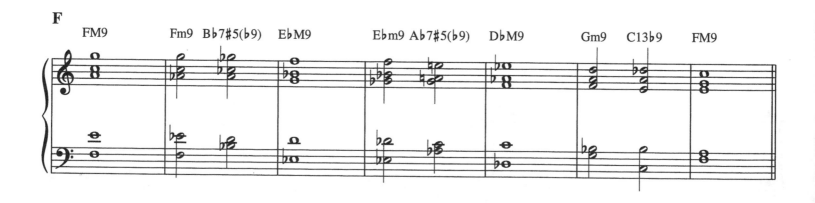

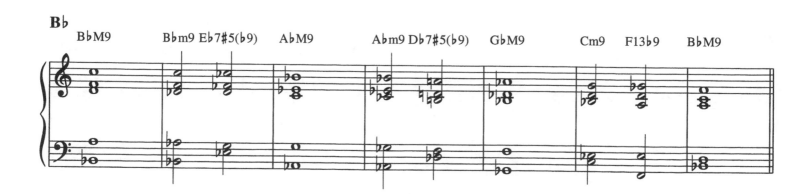

**Eb**

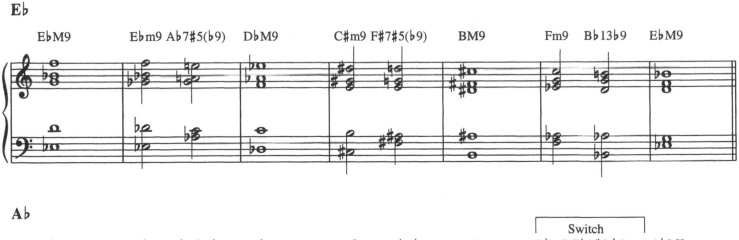

**Ab**

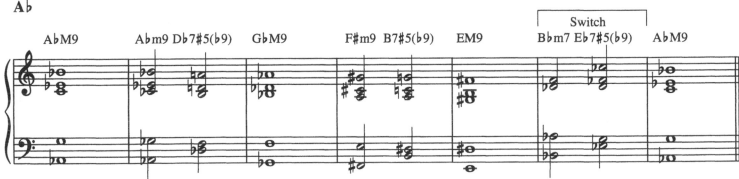

**Db**

Starting with Position 2:

**G**

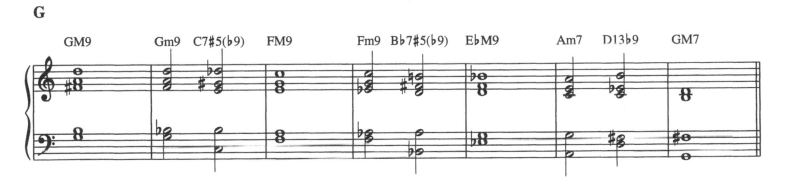

**C**

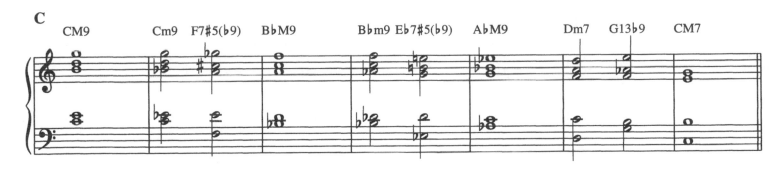

**F**

**B♭**

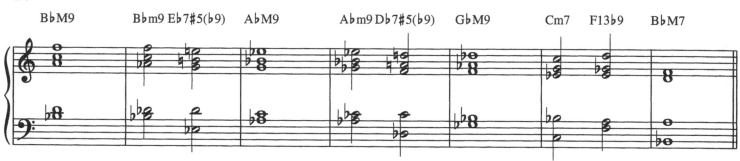

**E♭**

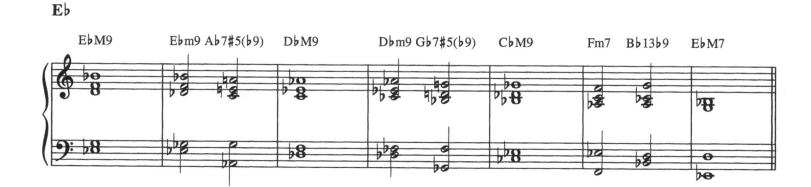

**A♭**

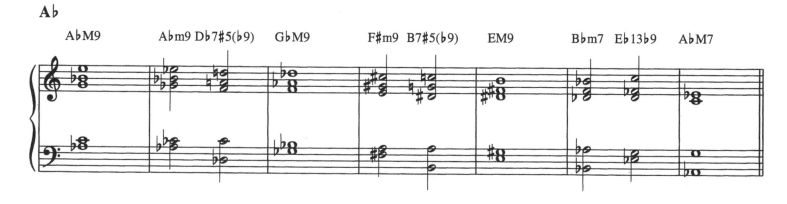

**D♭**

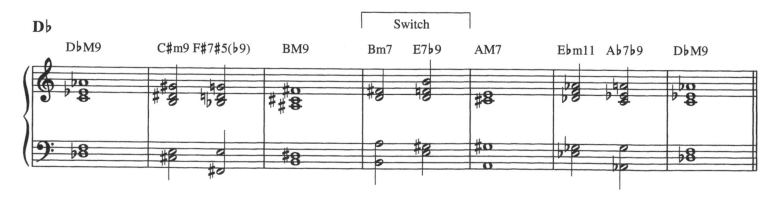

Miscellaneous chord progressions in the key of C Major:

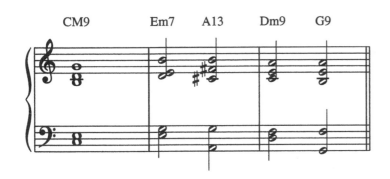

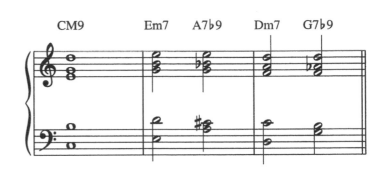

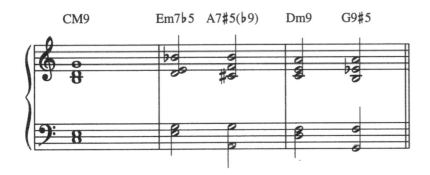

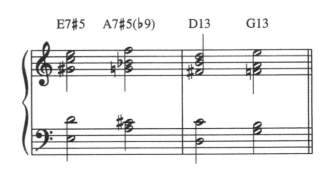

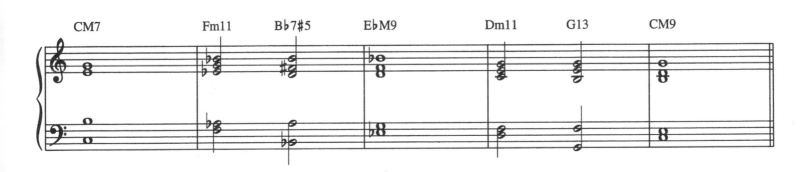

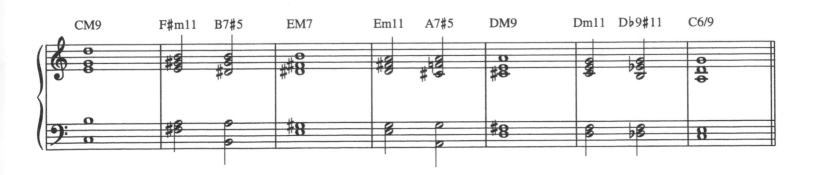

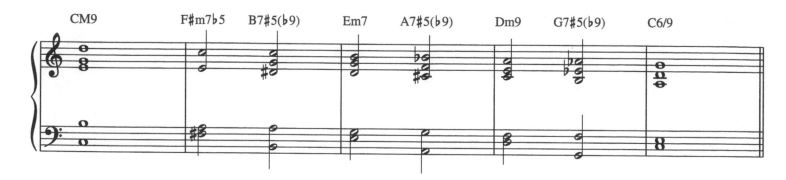

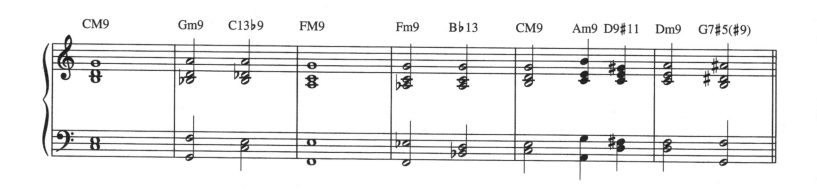

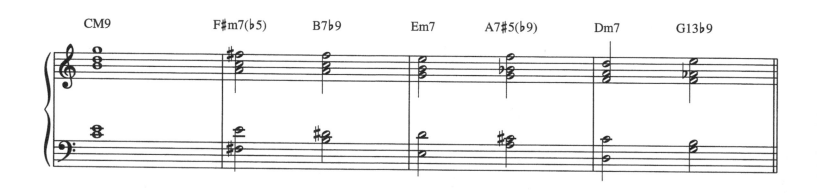

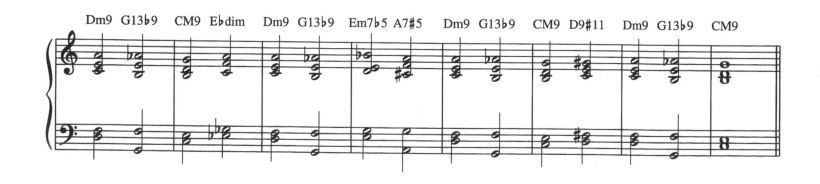

Memorize the II V I chord progression in all minor keys.

Starting with Position 1:

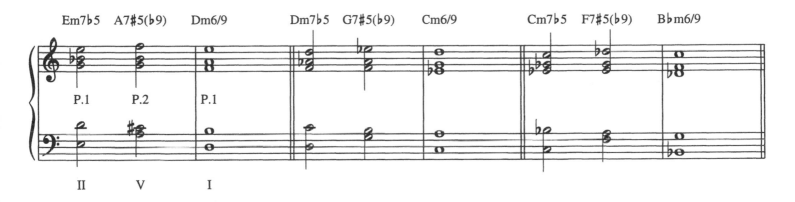

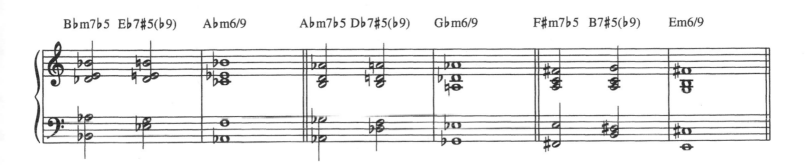

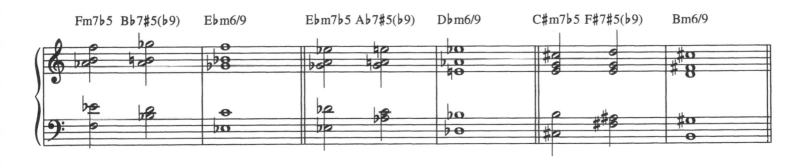

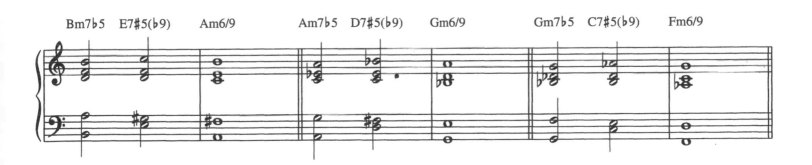

Starting with Position 2:

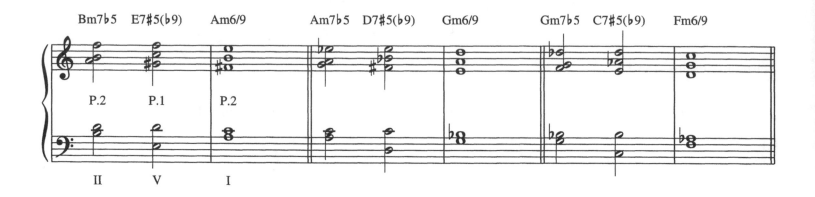

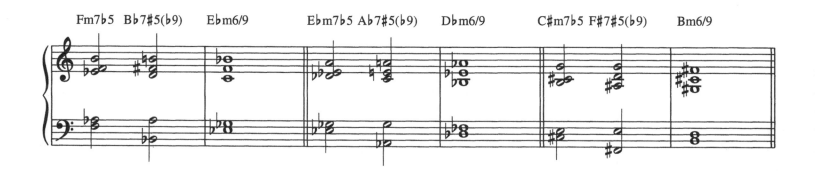

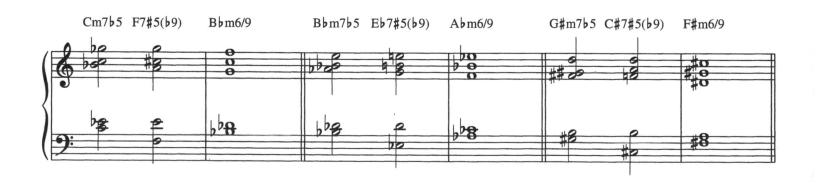

Only one example in each key appears below in order to avoid switching. Some examples start with Position 1 and others begin with Position 2. The more common keys of A, E and D minor replace the usual Eb, Ab and Db examples.

**Gm**

**Cm**

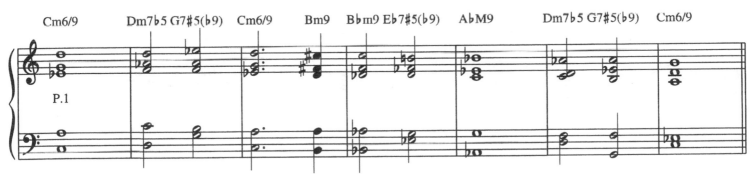

**Fm**

42

**Bbm**

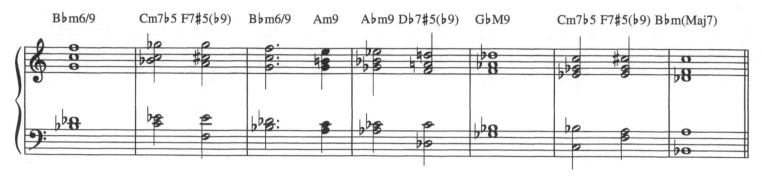

**Em**

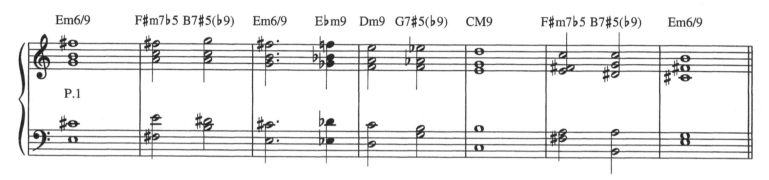

**Am**

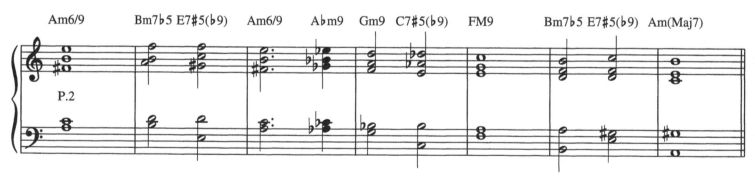

**Dm**

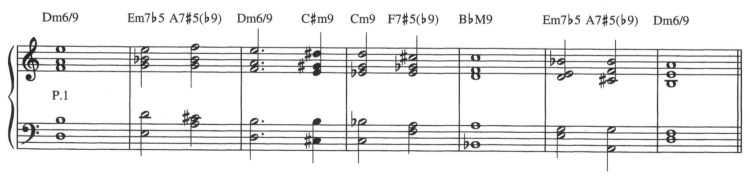

# 4. TURNAROUNDS

A turnaround is simply a 1st Ending, usually two measures, which begins with a I chord and progresses to some kind of dominant harmony in order to return to the I chord at the beginning of the song or improvisation. All of the progressions in this chapter could also appear anywhere in the song and are not restricted to turnarounds.

Another important jazz chord progression is I VI II V. The first four turnarounds are based on this progression.

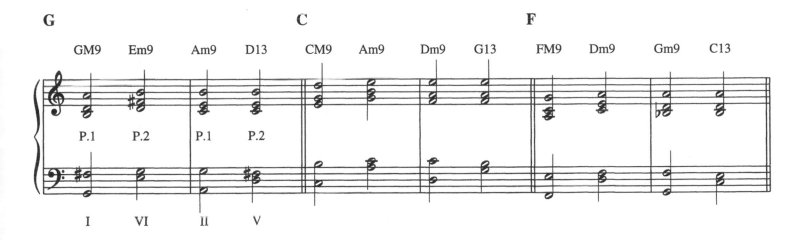

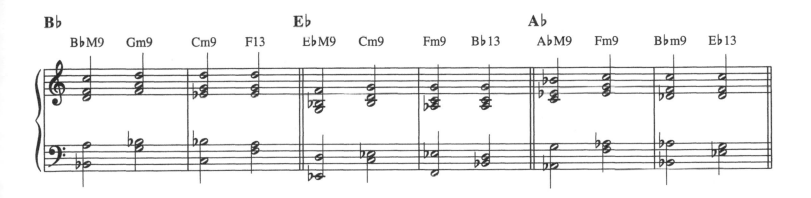

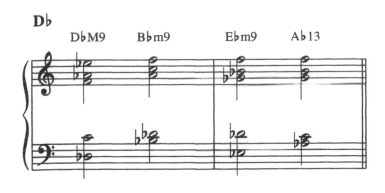

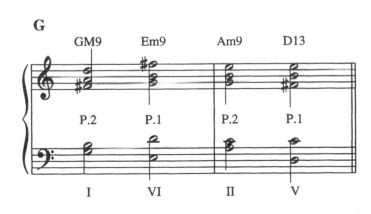

44

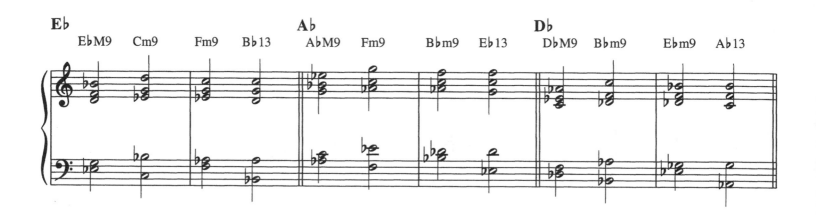

In the next progression the VI and II are dominant chords.

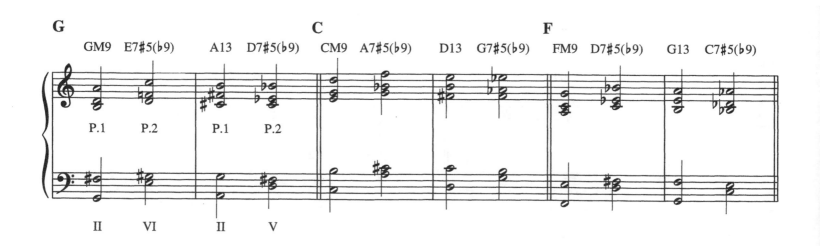

**Bb**

BbM9  G7#5(b9)  C13  F7#5(b9)

**Eb**

EbM9  C7#5(b9)  F13  Bb7#5(b9)

**Ab**

AbM9  F7#5(b9)  Bb13  Eb7#5(b9)

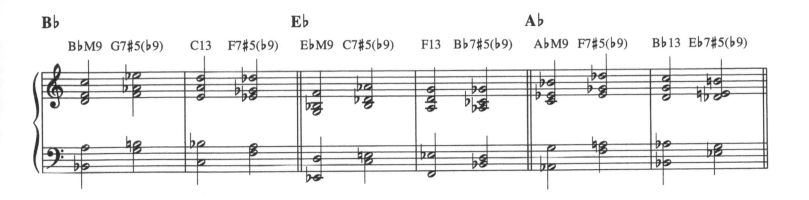

**Db**

DbM9  Bb7#5(b9)  Eb13  Ab7#5(b9)

**G**

GM9  E7#5(b9)  A9  D7#5(b9)

P.2  P.1  P.2  P.1

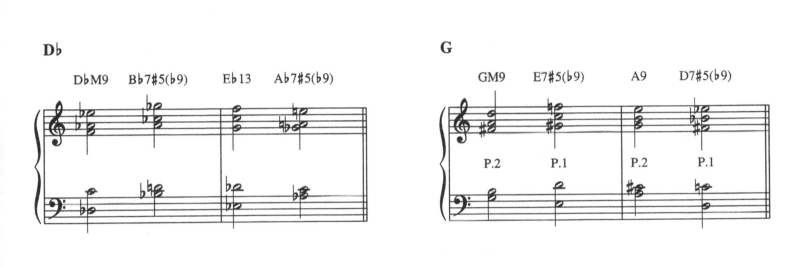

**C**

CM9  A7#5(b9)  D9  G7#5(b9)

**F**

FM9  D7#5(b9)  G9  C7#5(b9)

**Bb**

BbM9  G7#5(b9)  C9  F7#5(b9)

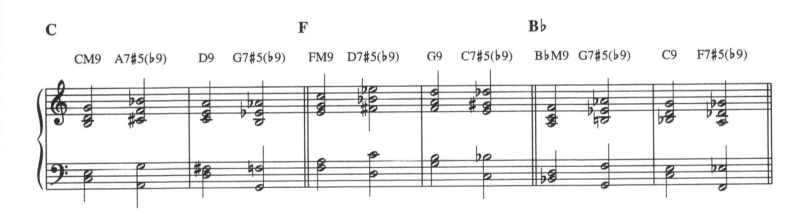

**Eb**

EbM9  C7#5(b9)  F9  Bb7#5(b9)

**Ab**

AbM9  F7#5(b9)  Bb9  Eb7#5(b9)

**Db**

DbM9  Bb7#5(b9)  Eb9  Ab7#5(b9)

The tri-tone substitution is applied to the VI and V chords.

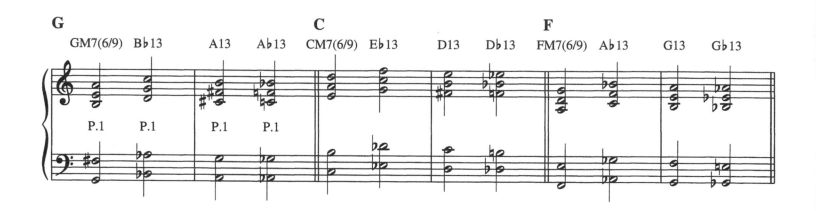

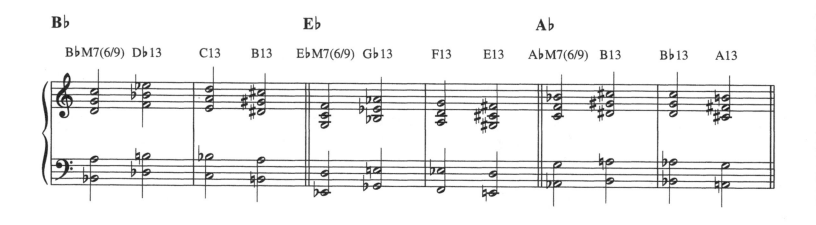

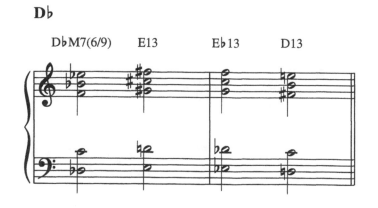

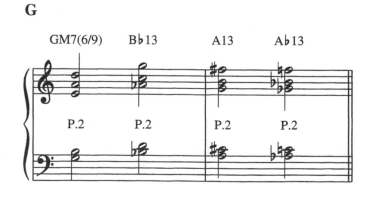

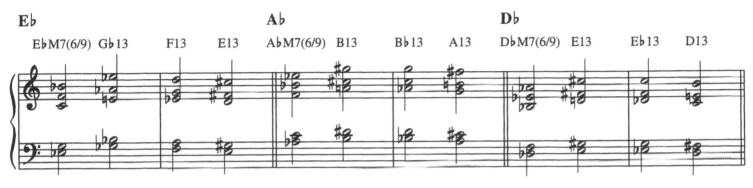

The tri-tone substitution is applied to every chord but the I chord. Notice that the substitute for the II chord (D) is a major seventh (AbM7).

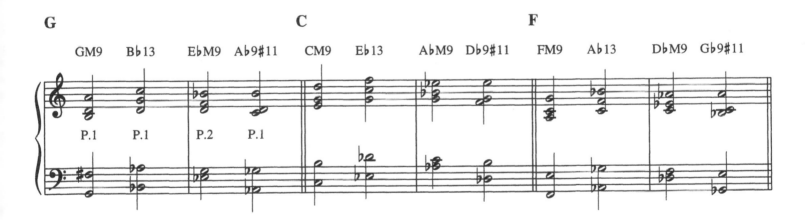

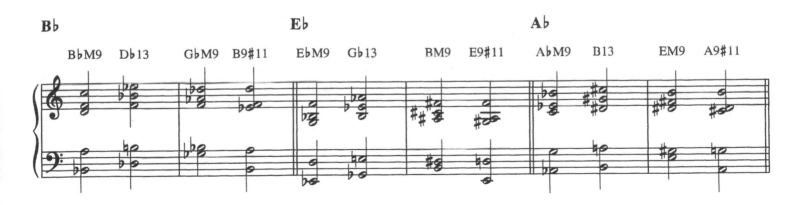

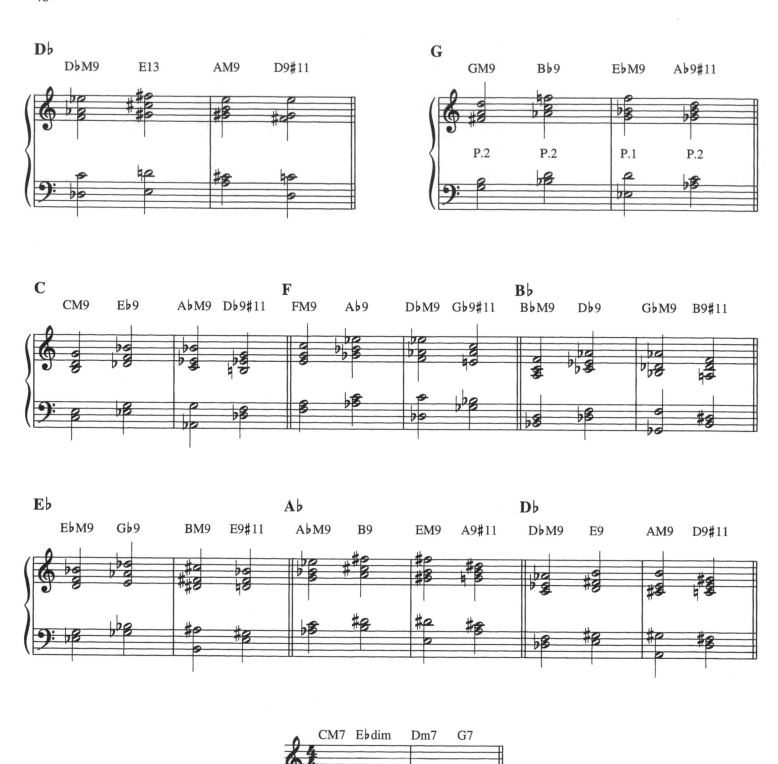

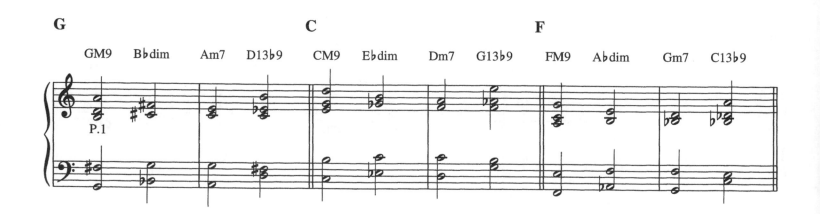

**B♭**

**D♭**

**G**

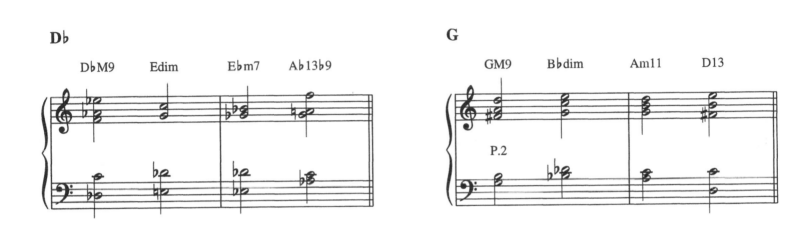

**C**

**F**

**B♭**

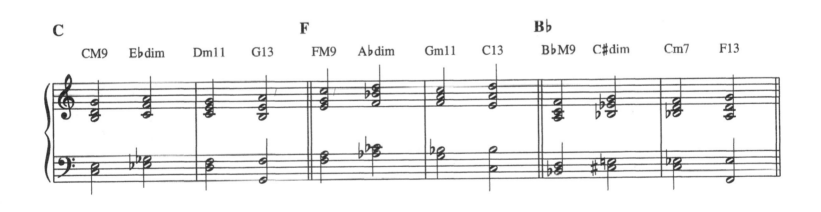

**E♭**

**A♭**

**D♭**

Miscellaneous turnarounds in the key of C Major:

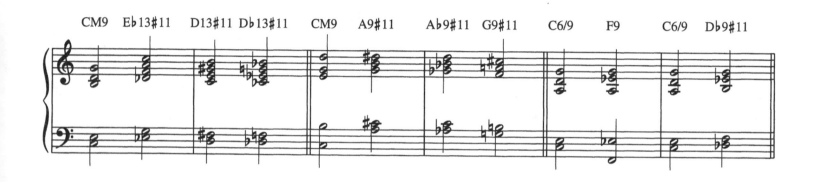

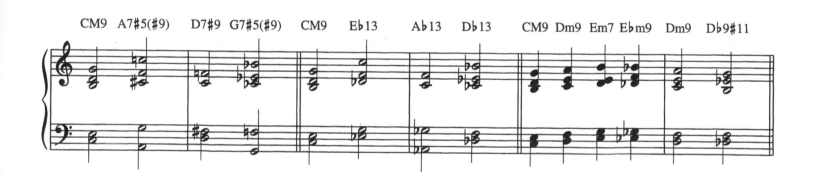

# 5. CHORD VOICINGS WITH THE 3RD OR 7TH AS THE BOTTOM NOTE

The 3rd is the bottom note in the left hand in Position 1. The 7th is the bottom note in the left hand in Position 2. Some of these voicings contain no root. This voicing is especially good when a bass player is playing the roots or a bass line.

## POSITION 1

**MAJOR:**

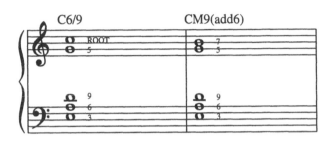

**MINOR:**

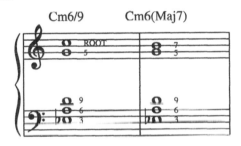

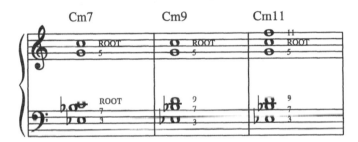

**DOMINANT SEVENTH:**          **DIMINISHED:**

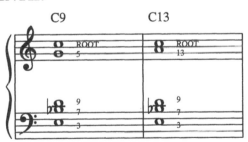

### ALTERED CHORDS

**MINOR:**

This voicing is an exception to the rule:

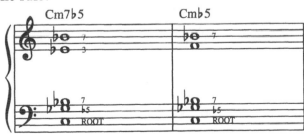

**DOMINANT SEVENTH:**

**DIMINISHED:**

The note which is one whole step above the 6th is added.

# POSITION 2

**MAJOR:**

## MINOR:

The m6 chord has the 6th as the lowest note in the left hand.

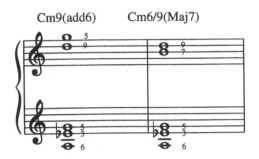

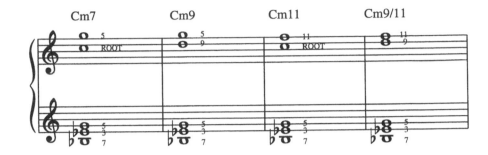

## DOMINANT SEVENTH:

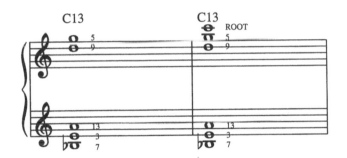

## DIMINISHED:

## ALTERED CHORDS

### MINOR:

Exception:

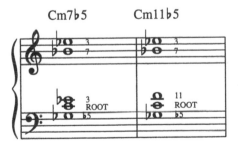

### DOMINANT SEVENTH:

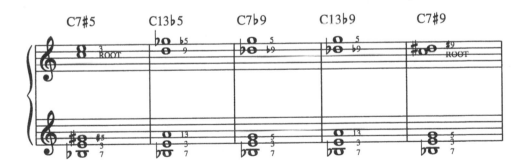

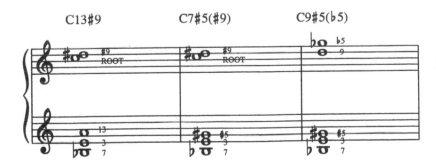

### DIMINISHED:

The note a whole step above the 5th is added.

# 6. CHORD PROGRESSIONS

The Position 1 and 2 chord voicings are applied to chord progressions. The position selection rules remain the same. The voicings for both positions should fall within the range indicated below.

Memorize the following II V I chord progression in all major keys.

Starting with Position 1:

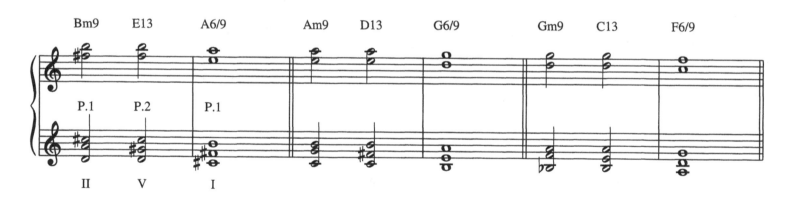

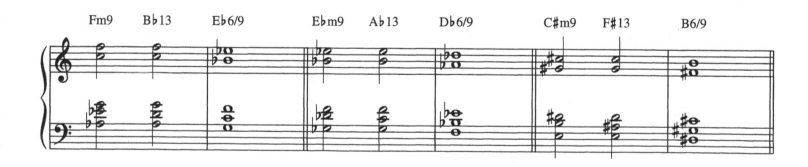

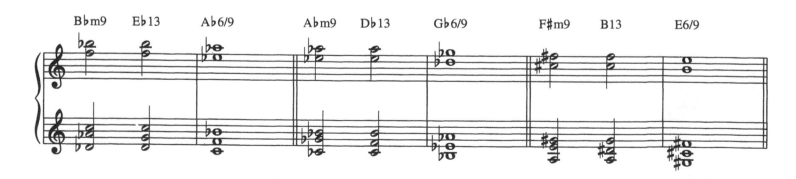

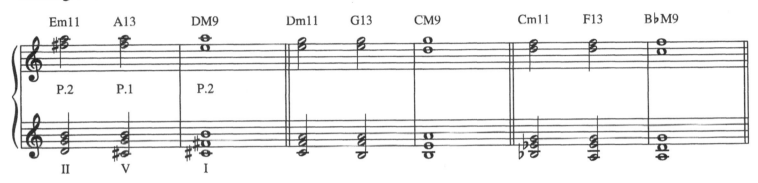

Starting with Position 2:

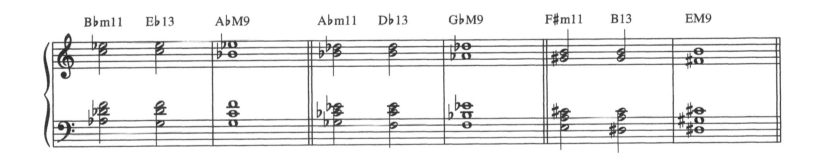

This progression often appears as the bridge in standard jazz tunes.

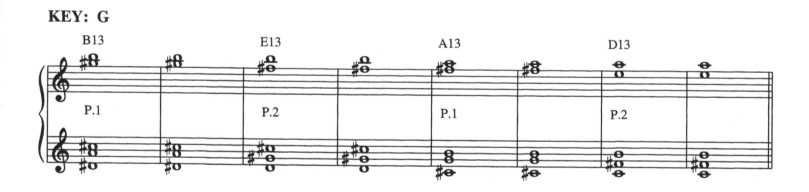

Starting with Position 1:

**KEY: G**

C

**F**

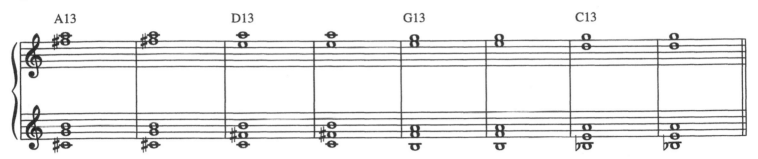

**B♭**

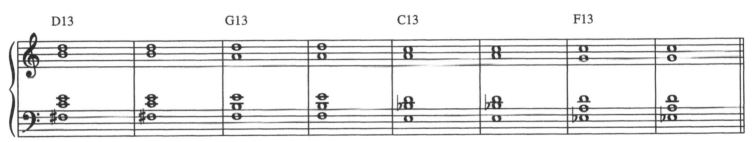

**E♭**

**A♭**

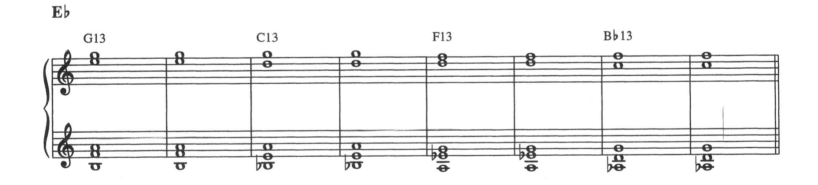

**Db**

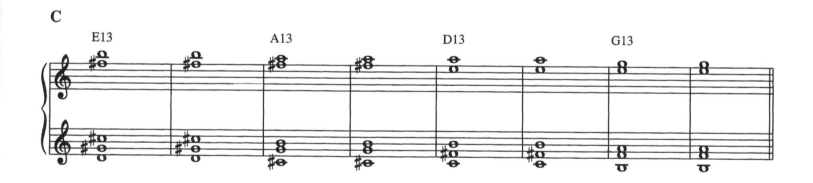

Starting with Position 2:

**G**

**C**

**F**

**B♭**

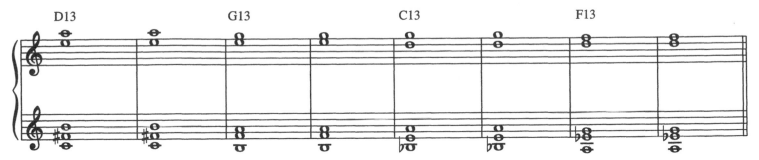

**E♭**

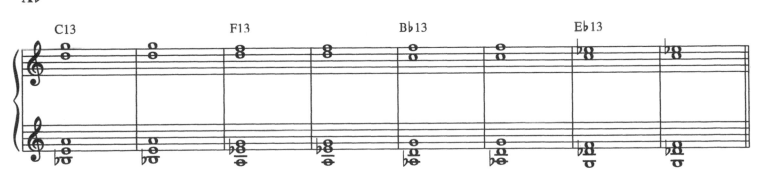

**A♭**

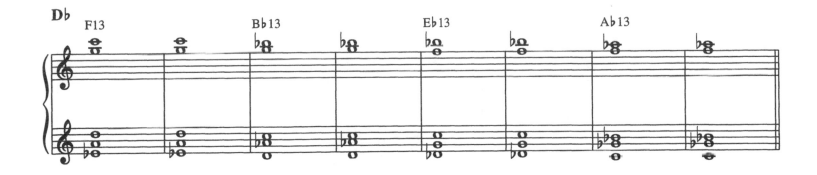

**D♭**

The following progression is the same as the preceding one. However, m7 chords have been placed before each dominant 7th chord to establish a temporary II V relationship.

Starting with Position 1:

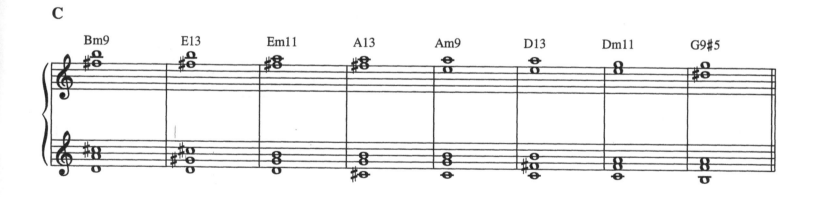

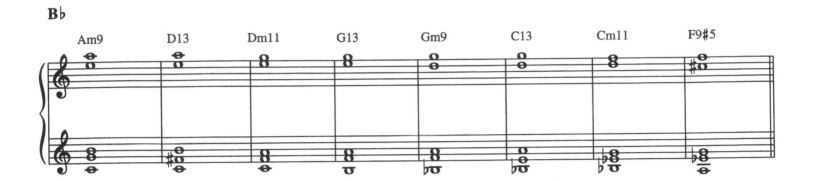

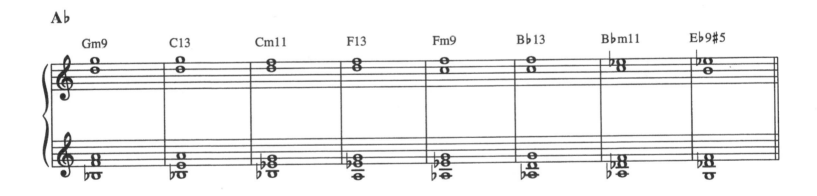

**B♭**

Am9    D13    Dm11    G13    Gm9    C13    Cm11    F9♯5

**E♭**

Dm9    G13    Gm11    C13    Cm9    F13    Fm11    B♭9♯5

**A♭**

Gm9    C13    Cm11    F13    Fm9    B♭13    B♭m11    E♭9♯5

Switch

**D♭**

Cm9    F13    Fm11    B♭13    B♭m11    E♭13    E♭m9    A♭13♭9

62

Starting with Position 2:

**G**

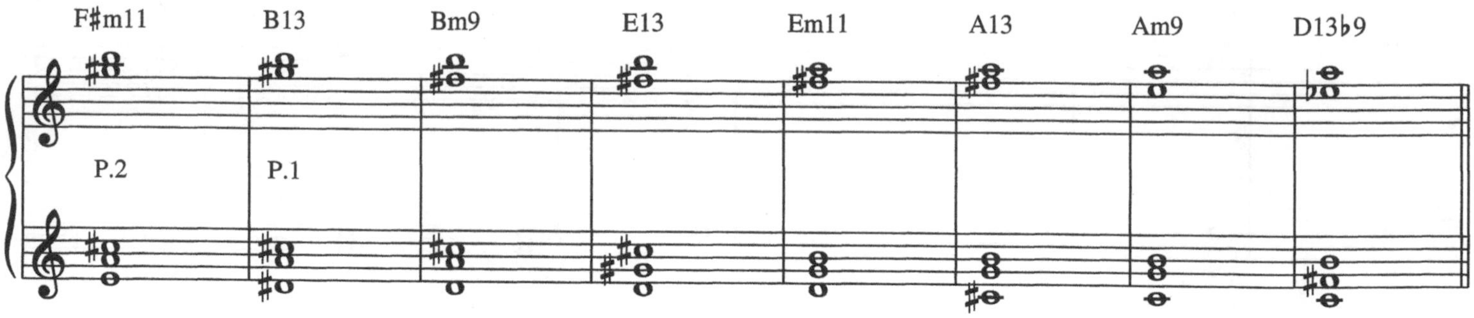

| F#m11 | B13 | Bm9 | E13 | Em11 | A13 | Am9 | D13b9 |

P.2    P.1

**C**

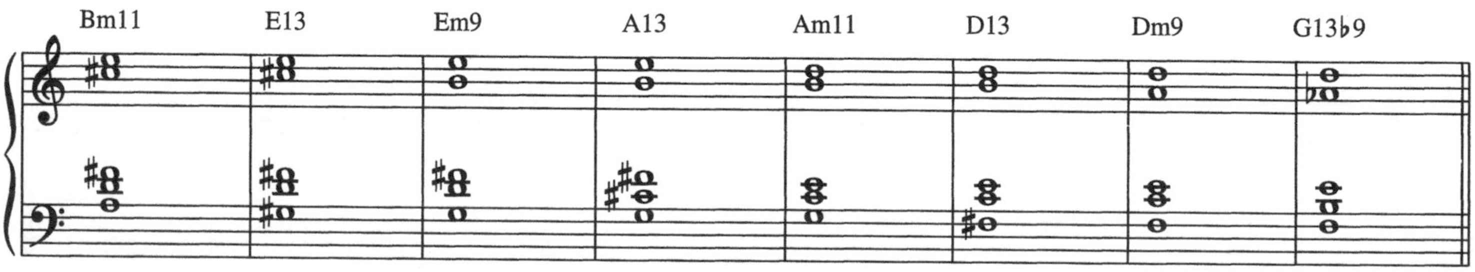

| Bm11 | E13 | Em9 | A13 | Am11 | D13 | Dm9 | G13b9 |

**F**

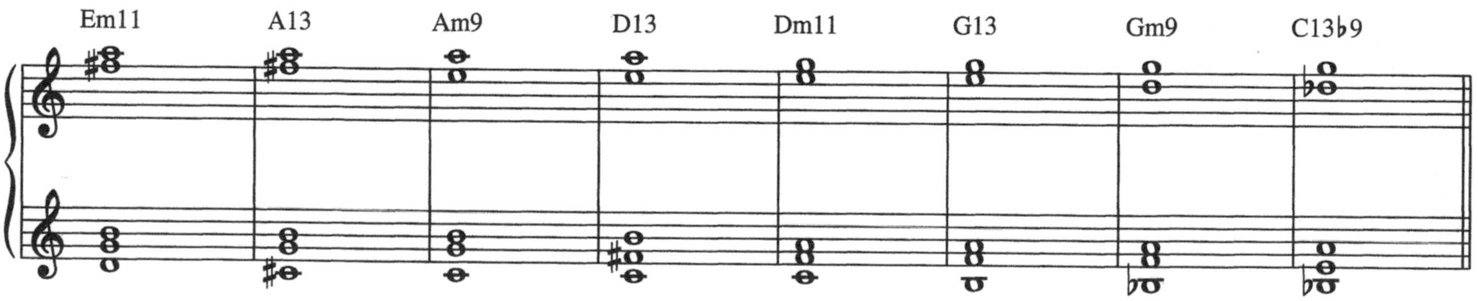

| Em11 | A13 | Am9 | D13 | Dm11 | G13 | Gm9 | C13b9 |

**Bb**

| Am11 | D13 | Dm9 | G13 | Gm11 | C13 | Cm9 | F13b9 |

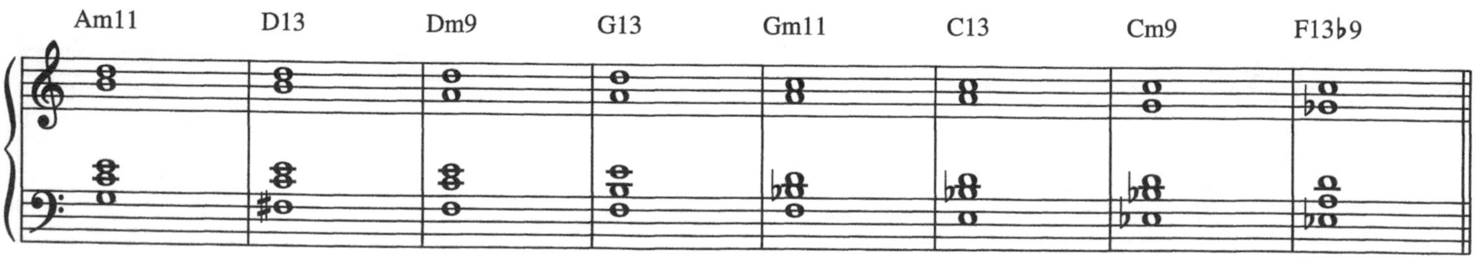

Another method of enhancing a series of dominant 7th chords follows. Dominant 7th chords one half step above and below the original chord are added.

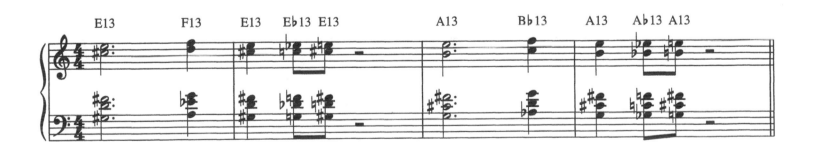

In the next chord progression the tri-tone substitution is applied to the A7 and G7 chords. (See Chapter 1)

Notice the second chord in measure three. The top voice doubles one of the notes in the left hand. Occasionally one note in the right hand may double a left hand note. Remember that a 13 ♭5 (C13♭5) may be written as a 7 ♯11 (C7♯11).

Starting with Position 1:

**G**

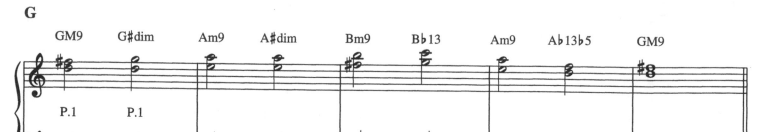

**C**

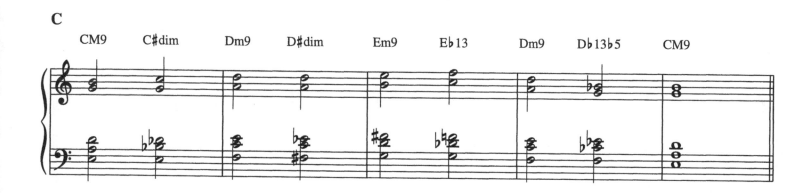

**F**

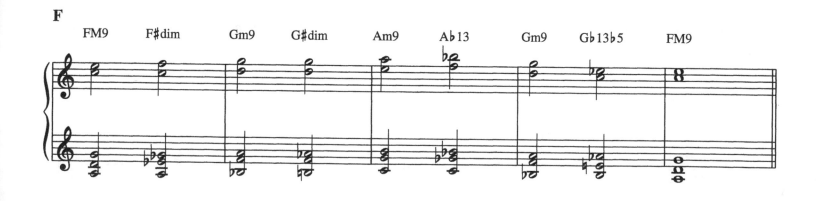

**B♭**

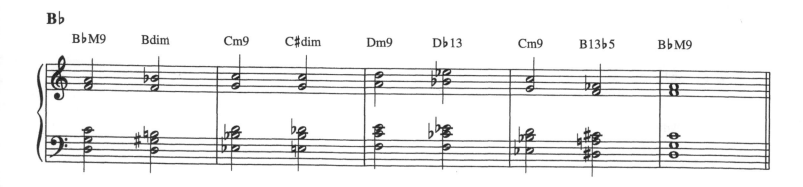

**E♭**

**A♭**

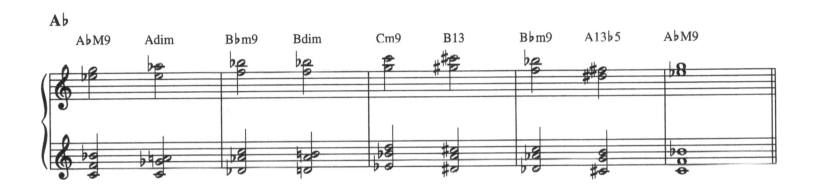

**D♭**

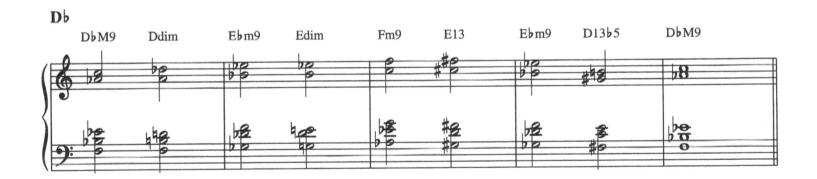

Starting with Position 2:

**G**

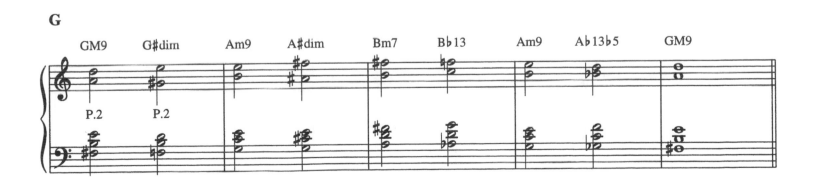

66

**C**

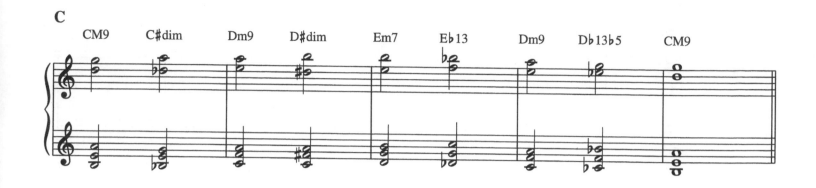

**F**

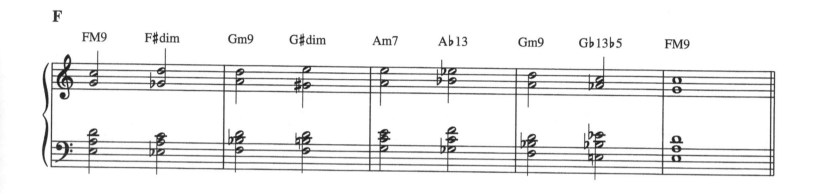

**B♭**

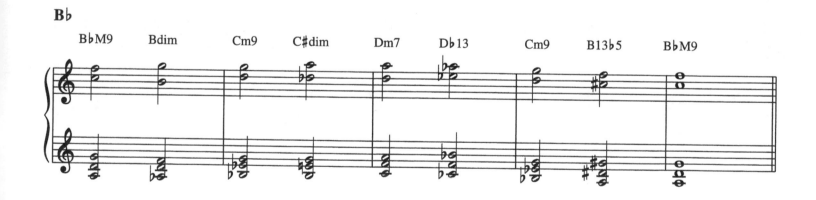

**E♭**

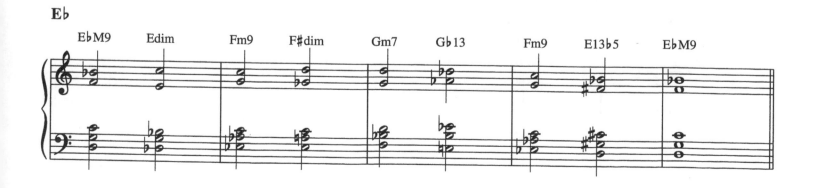

**Ab**

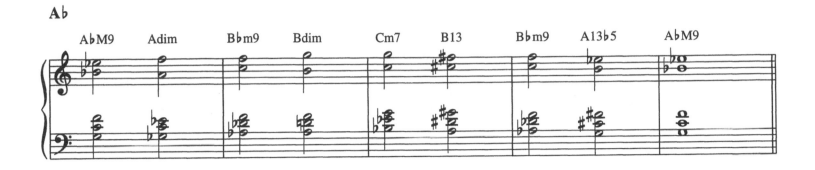

**Db**

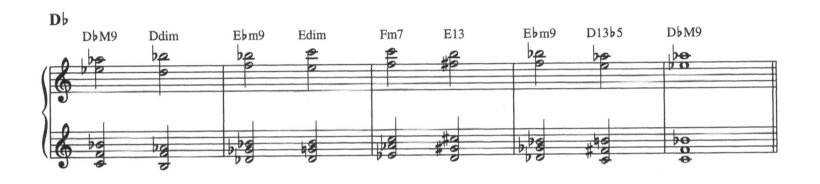

Starting with Position 1:

**G**

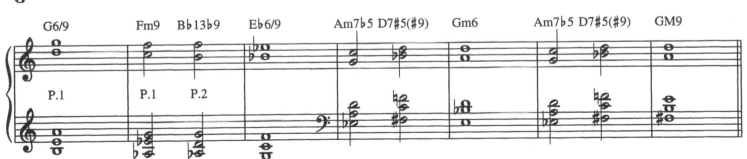

**C**

C6/9　　　Bbm9　Eb13b9　　Ab6/9　　　Dm7b5　G7#5(#9)　Cm6/9　　　Dm7b5　G7#5(#9)　CM9

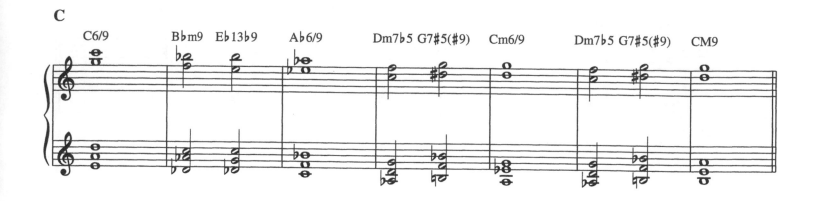

**F**

F6/9　　　Ebm9　Ab13b9　　Db6/9　　　Gm7b5　C7#5(#9)　Fm6/9　　　Gm7b5　C7#5(#9)　FM9

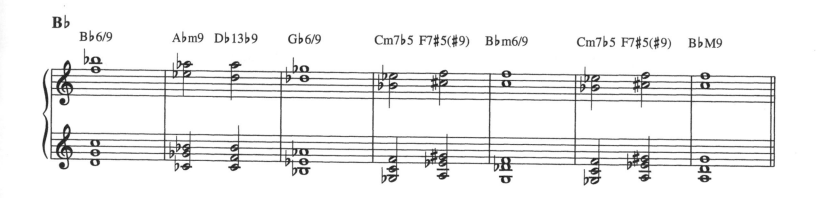

**Bb**

Bb6/9　　　Abm9　Db13b9　　Gb6/9　　　Cm7b5　F7#5(#9)　Bbm6/9　　　Cm7b5　F7#5(#9)　BbM9

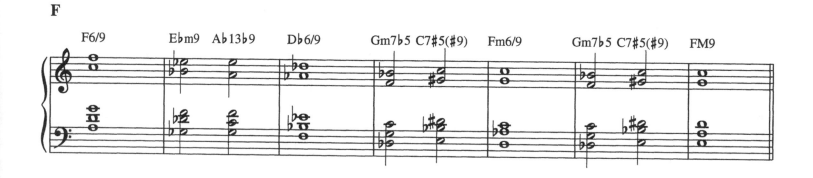

**Eb**

Eb6/9　　　C#m9　F#13b9　　B6/9　　　Fm7b5　Bb7#5(#9)　Ebm6/9　　　Fm7b5　Bb7#5(#9)　EbM9

Switch

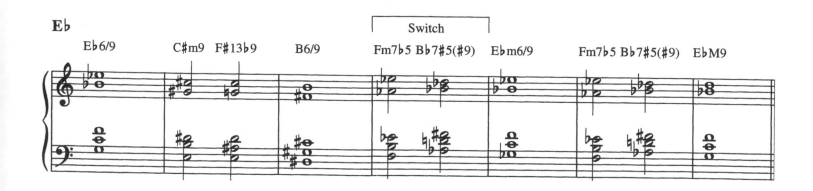

**A♭**

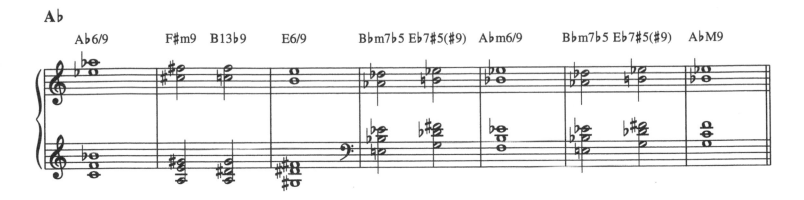

**D♭**

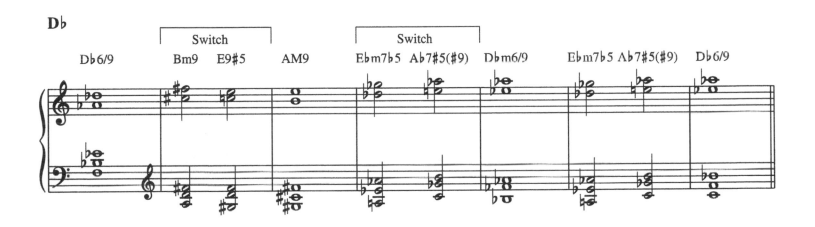

Starting with Position 2:

**G**

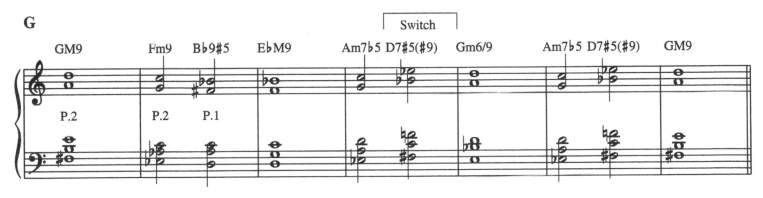

**C**

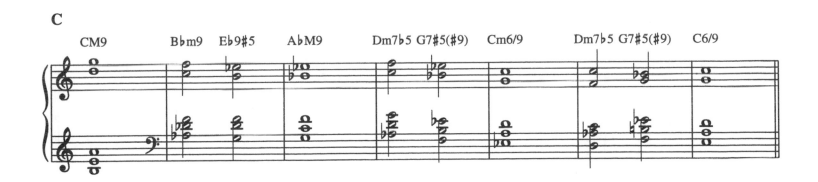

**F**

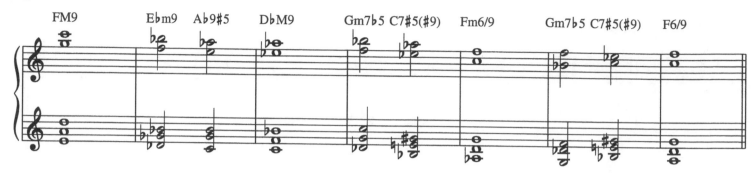

**B♭**

**E♭**

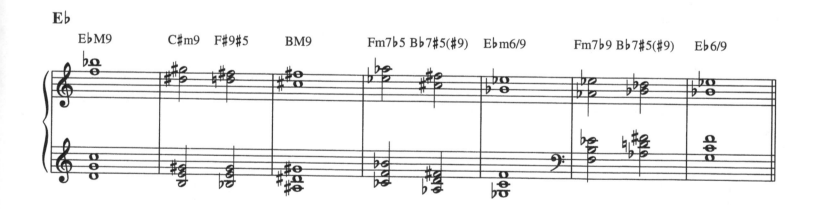

**A♭**

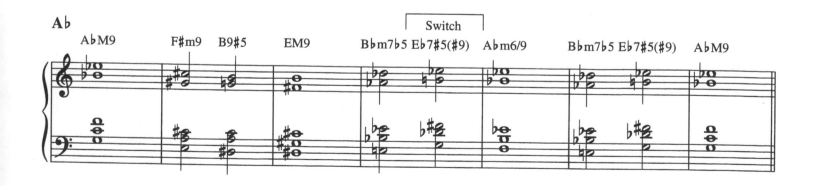

**D♭**

Add a ninth measure to this chord progression on your own. Play a IM9 chord in Position 2.

Ninth measure in Key of C Major:

Starting with Position 1:

**G**

**C**

**F**

**Bb**

**Eb**

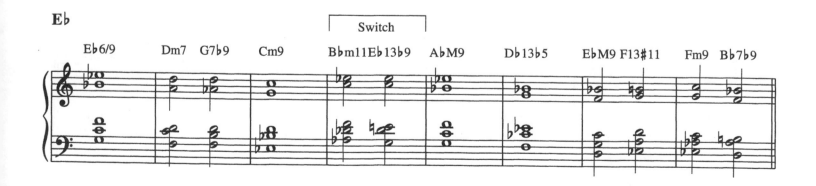

**A♭**

**D♭**

Starting with Position 2:

The following examples present this chord progression starting with Position 2 of the I chord which is a voicing with no root. When you are practicing a progression which begins with a rootless voicing, the key center is not clearly established in your ear. In this practice situation it is helpful to play a simple I chord triad before beginning the progression. In practical playing the root would be played by the bass player.

Add a ninth measure to the following progressions on your own. Play a I6/9 chord in Position 1 for all keys except G and A♭. Play a IM9 chord for the keys of G and A♭ in Position 2.

Ninth measure in Key of C Major:

**G**

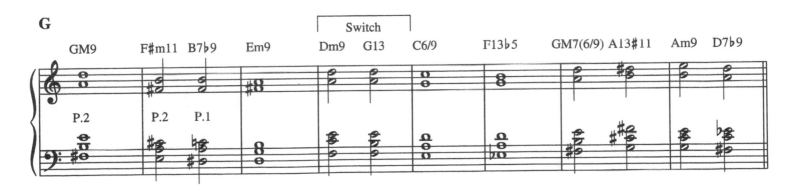

**C**

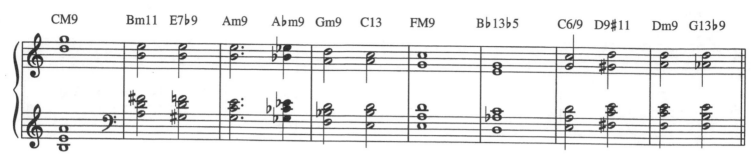

**F**

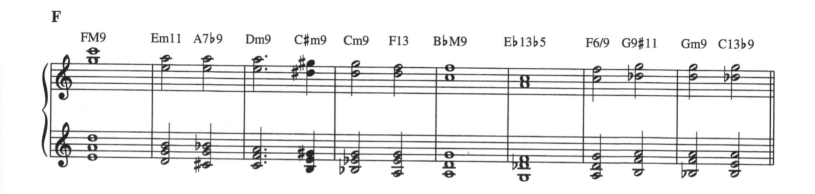

**B♭**

**E♭**

**Ab**

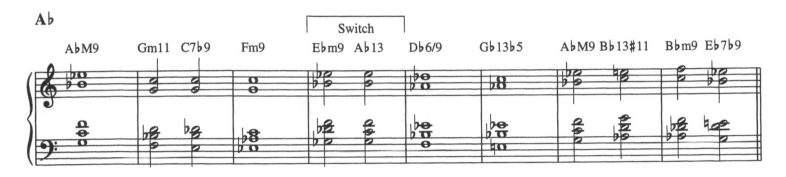

**Db**

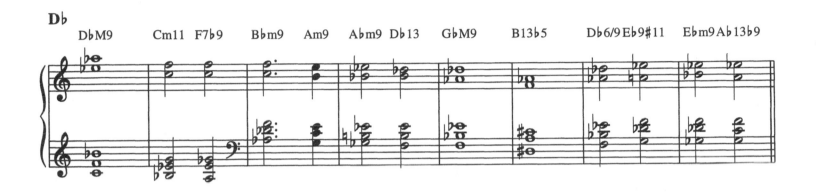

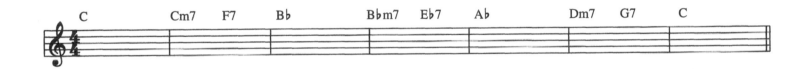

Starting with Position 1:

**G**

**C**

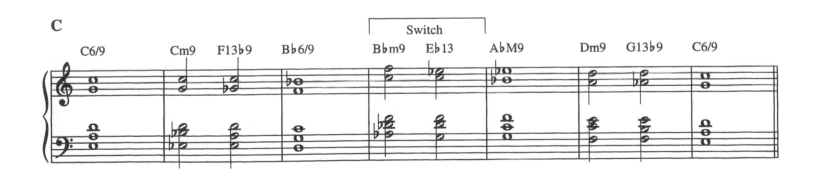

**F**

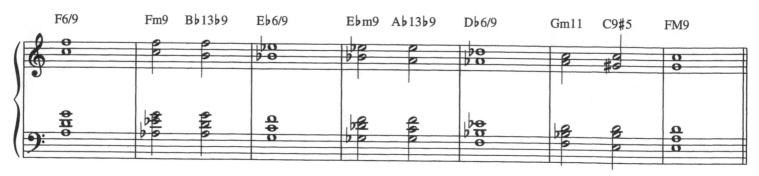

**B♭**

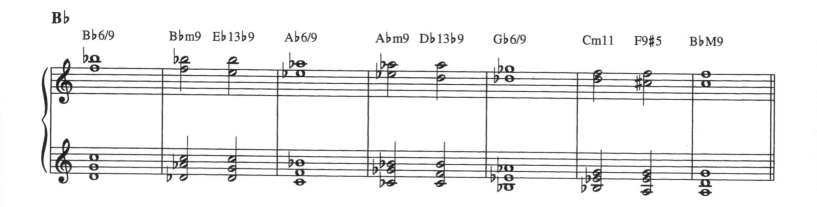

**E♭**

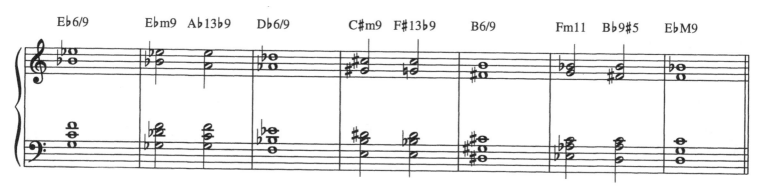

**A♭**

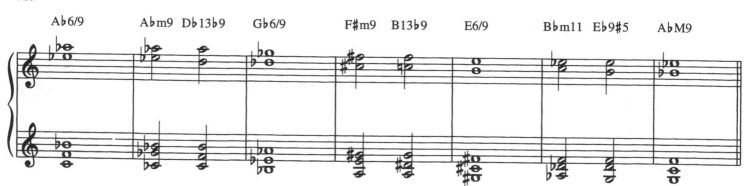

**D♭**

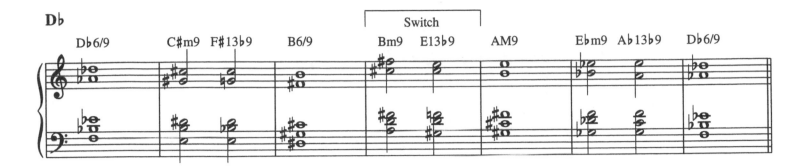

**Starting with Position 2:**

Notice the 7♯5♯9 chords on the third beat of measures two and four. Because of the tri-tone substitution rule, the roots for these chords could be the note a tri-tone away. In the key of C example the F7 could be a B7 and the E♭ could be an A7. Think about this when playing the following examples.

**G**

**C**

**F**

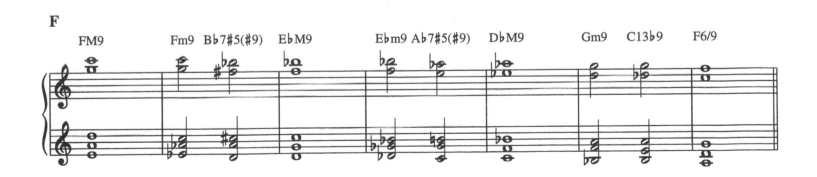

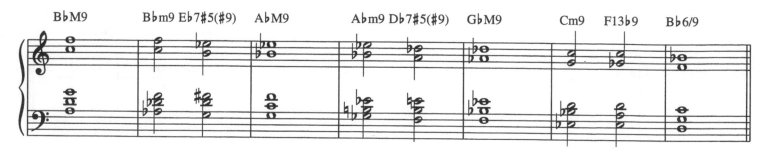

78

**B♭**

**E♭**

**A♭**

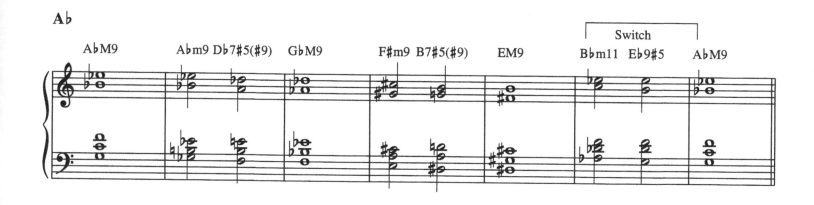

**D♭**

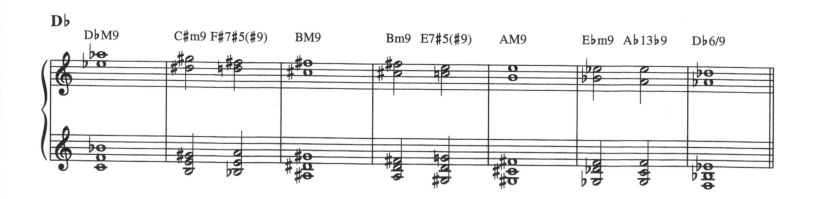

Miscellaneous chord progressions in the key of C Major:

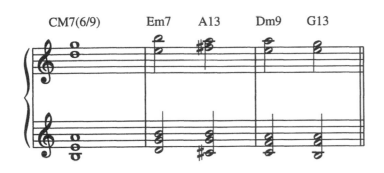

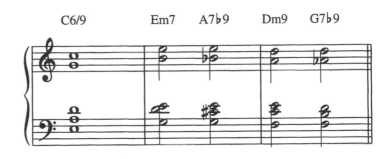

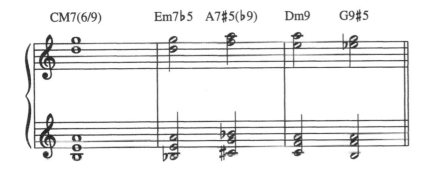

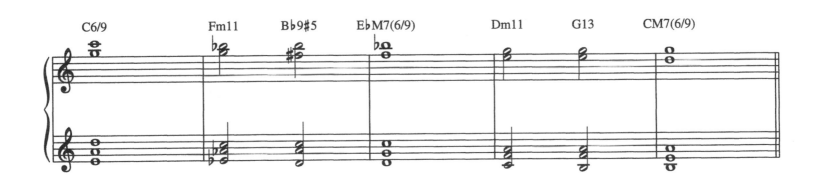

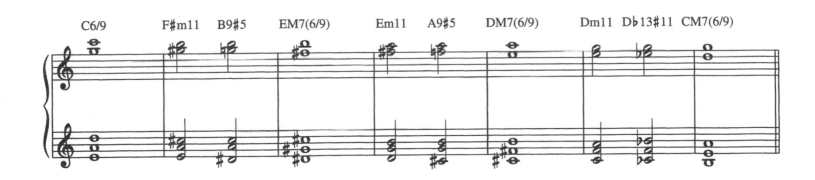

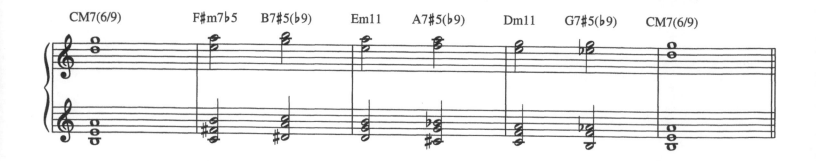

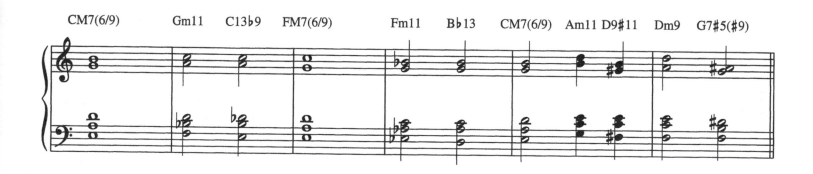

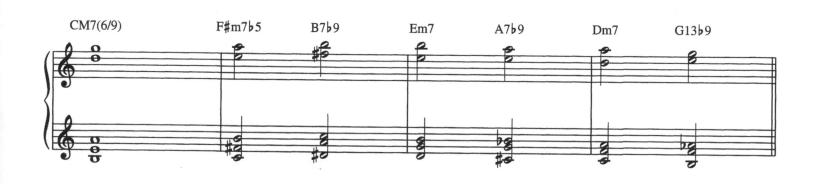

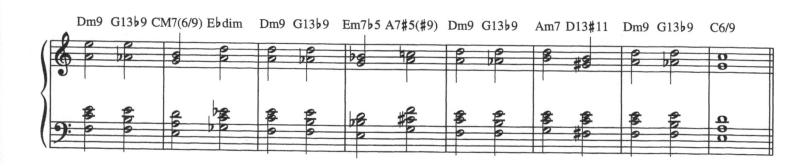

Memorize the II V I chord progression in all minor keys.

Starting with the first position of the m7♭5 chord:
(Remember that the m7♭5 chord is an exception to the position rule.)

Starting with the second position of the m7♭5 chord:

The V7 chord symbol in this progression is written "alt." (G7alt.). This chord is a 7♯5♭9♯9 (G7♯5♭9♯9). The symbol for a chord with many altered notes is often written "alt." (G7alt.). This designation simplifies the chord symbol for a complicated chord structure.

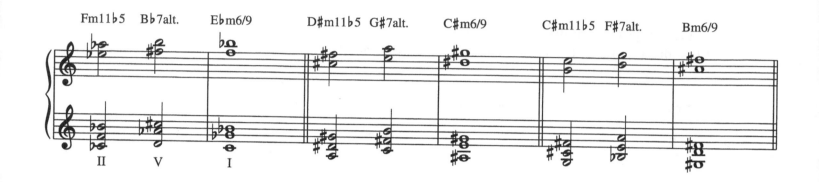

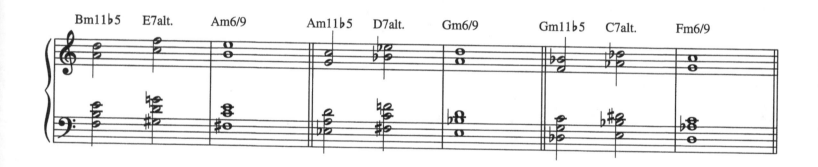

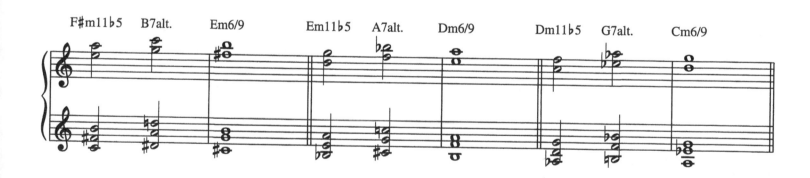

C    Dm7♭5   G7    Cm    Bm7    B♭m7    E♭7    A♭M7    Dm7♭5   G7    Cm

Only one example in each key appears below in order to avoid switching. Some examples start with Position 1 and others begin with Position 2. The more common keys of A, E and D minor replace the usual E♭, A♭ and D♭ examples.

**Gm**

**Cm**

**Fm**

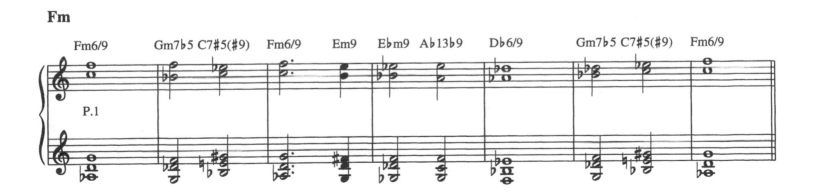

**B♭m**

**Em**

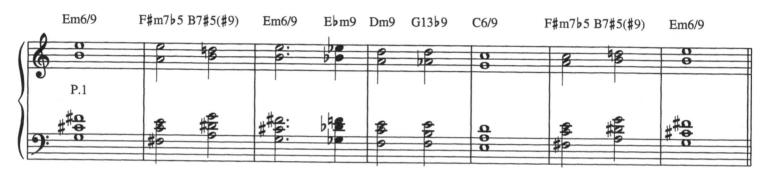

**Am**

**Dm**

# 7. TURNAROUNDS

The first four turnarounds are based on the I VI II V chord progression. This progression may also appear anywhere in the song.

**G**

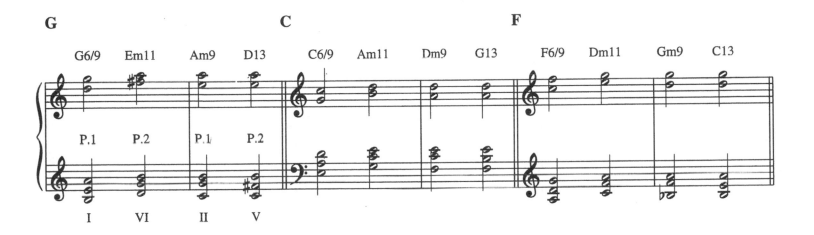

**Bb**

**Db**

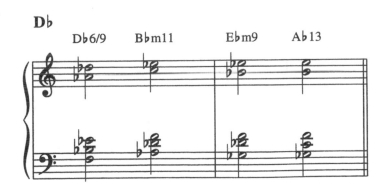

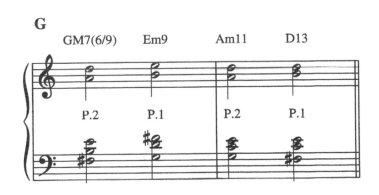

In the next progression the VI and II are dominant chords.

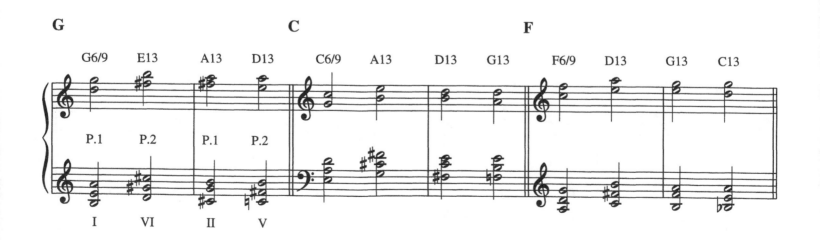

**B♭**

Bb6/9  G13      C13   F13

**E♭**

Eb6/9  C13      F13   Bb13

**A♭**

Ab6/9  F13      Bb13  Eb13

**D♭**

Db6/9  Bb13   Eb13   Ab13

**G**

GM7(6/9)  E13    Am13   D13

P.2      P.1     P.2    P.1

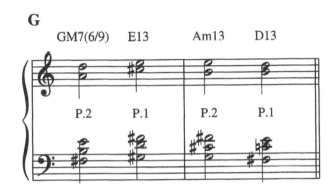

**C**

CM7(6/9)  A13    D13   G13

**F**

FM7(6/9)  D13    G13   C13

**B♭**

BbM7(6/9)  G13   C13   F13

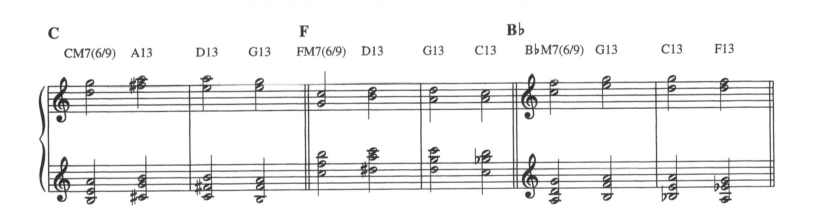

**E♭**

EbM7(6/9)  C13    F13   Bb13

**A♭**

AbM7(6/9)  F13    Bb13  Eb13

**D♭**

DbM7(6/9)  Bb13   Eb13  Ab13

The tri-tone substitution is applied to the VI and V chords.

The tri-tone substitution is applied to every chord but the I chord. The substitute for the II chord is a major 7th (AbM7). On the Db7 chord a note is added to the top of the voicing which doubles the top note in the left hand.

**Db**

Db6/9   E13      AM7(6/9) D13#11

**G**

GM7(6/9)  Bb13     EbM7(6/9) Ab13#11

P.2       P.2      P.1      P.2

**C**                                      **F**                                           **Bb**

CM7(6/9) Eb13   AbM7(6/9) Db13#11   FM7(6/9) Ab13    DbM7(6/9) Gb13#11   BbM7(6/9) Db13   GbM7(6/9) B13#11

**Eb**                              **Ab**                              **Db**

EbM7(6/9) Gb13   BM7(6/9) E13#11   AbM7(6/9) B13   EM7(6/9) A13#11   DbM7(6/9) E13   AM7(6/9) D13#11

C   Ebdim    Dm7   G7

**G**                                      **C**                                           **F**

G6/9   Bbdim   Am9   D13b9    C6/9   Ebdim   Dm9   G13b9    F6/9   Abdim   Gm9   C13b9

P.1

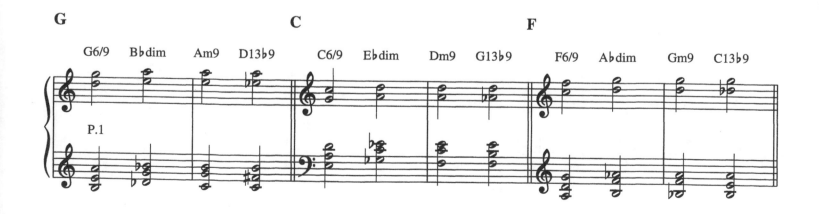

**B♭**

Bb6/9    Dbdim    Cm9    F13b9    Eb6/9    Gbdim    Fm9    Bb13b9

**E♭**

**A♭**

Ab6/9    Bdim    Bbm9    Eb13b9

**D♭**

Db6/9    Edim    Ebm9    Ab13b9

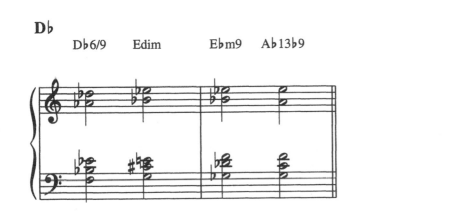

**G**

GM7(6/9)    Bbdim    Am11    D13

P.2

**C**

CM7(6/9)    Ebdim    Dm11    G13

**F**

FM7(6/9)    Abdim    Gm11    C13

**B♭**

BbM7(6/9)    Dbdim    Cm11    F13

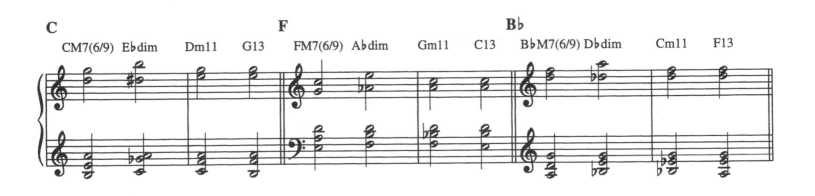

**E♭**

EbM7(6/9)    Gbdim    Fm11    Bb13

**A♭**

AbM7(6/9)    Bdim    Bbm11    Eb13

**D♭**

DbM7(6/9)    Edim    Ebm11    Ab13

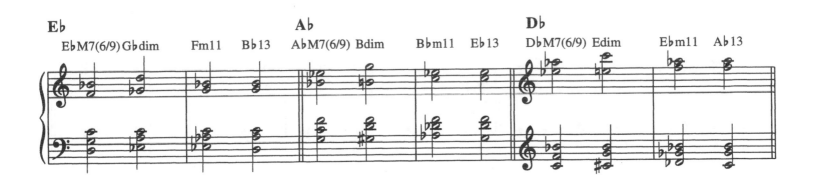

Miscellaneous turnarounds in the key of C Major:

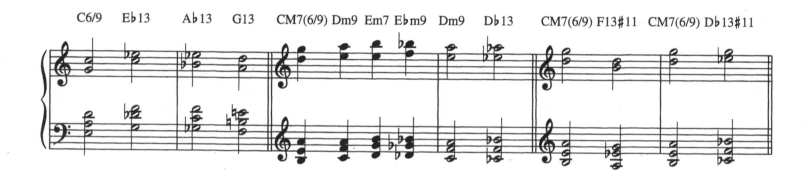

This voicing is quite versatile as just about any chord tone, or altered note that sounds well may be played in the right hand in any order.  The right hand may occasionally double a note in the left hand.  The examples below illustrate this voicing.  Notice the notes are more spread out.  The third example is in the key of G major to avoid switching.

# 8. FOURTH VOICINGS

Fourth voicings occur when either all the intervals in the chord structure are perfect fourths or all but one of the intervals is a perfect fourth.

Minor 11 and dominant 7th suspended chords are often played with fourth voicings.

## MINOR 11TH:

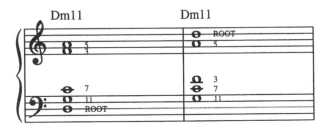

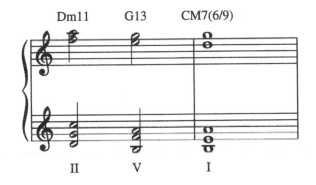

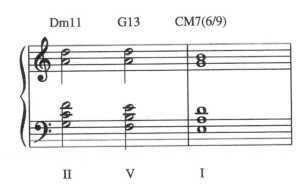

## DOMINANT 7TH SUSPENDED:

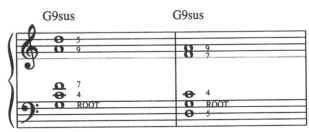

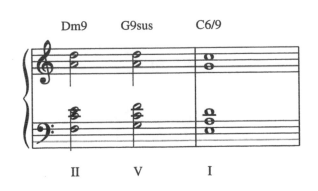

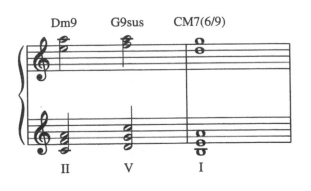

Notice that the voicings for the two chords are identical. The following examples show that the voicing for the two chords may remain the same in a progression. The root movement, played by the bass player, will determine the chord.

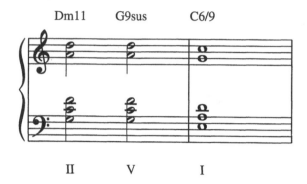 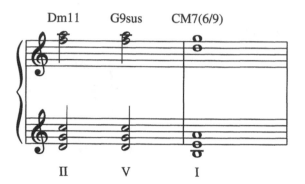

The voicings for the major chord work well in this situation because they are also fourth voicings.

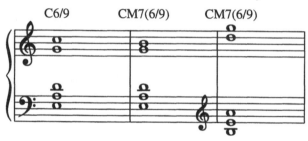

These chord structures may move up or down a whole or half step quickly without changing the basic chord sound.

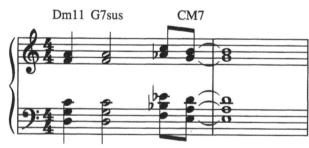

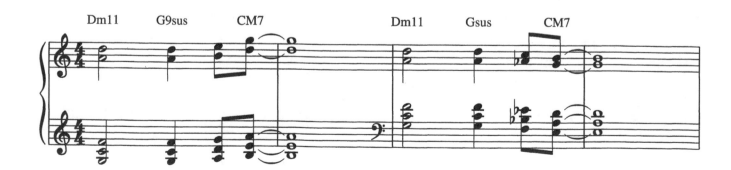

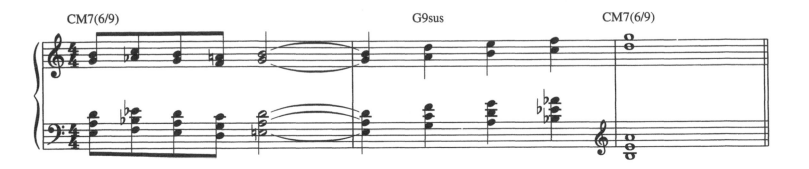

When the m11 and the dominant 7th sus are played together in a progression, they blend into one overall sound. These voicings are sometimes called MODAL voicings. They are applied to modal compositions when the m11 chord is played for the entire chorus. The following example illustrates a modal progression.

When the following m11 chord voicing moves up a whole step and back, it may be applied to a IIm7 V7 progression.

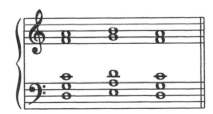

The above voicing is applied to the chord progression of a famous jazz standard tune: